THE SMART BAKING COOKBOOK

Muffins, Cookies, Biscuits, and Breads

OTHER NEWMARKET TITLES
BY JANE KINDERLEHRER

Smart Cookies
Smart Muffins
Smart Breakfasts
Smart Chicken
Smart Fish

THE SMART BAKING COOKBOOK

Muffins, Cookies, Biscuits, and Breads

JANE KINDERLEHRER

NEWMARKET PRESS

New York

First Edition

10 9 8 7 6 5 4 3 2 1

Library of Congress Cataloging-in-Publication Data
Kinderlehrer, Jane.
  The smart baking cookbook : muffins, cookies, biscuits, and
breads / Jane Kinderlehrer.
      p.   cm.
  Includes index.
  ISBN 1-55704-281-0
  1. Baked products. 2. High-fiber diet—Recipes. 3. Low-fat
diet—Recipes. 4. Sugar—free diet—Recipes. I. Title.
TX763.K53   1996   96-8662
641.8'15—dc20   CIP

Quantity Purchases
Companies, professional groups, clubs, and other organizations may qualify
for special terms when ordering quantities of this title. For information, write
Special Sales, Newmarket Press, 18 East 48th Street, New York, NY 10017,
or call (212) 832-3575, or fax (212) 832-3629.

Manufactured in the United States of America

Dedicated with much love and great joy to
Abraham Joseph Allen
whose arrival in January 1997
made us very happy
Great Grandparents

CONTENTS

METRIC CONVERSION CHART

1 teaspoon = 5 ml.   1 tablespoon = 15 ml.

1 ounce = 30 ml.   1 cup = 240 ml./.24 l.

1 quart = 950 ml./.95 l.   1 gallon = 3.80 l.

1 ounce = 28 gr.   1 pound = 454 gr./.454 kg.

F°	200	225	250	275	300	325	350	375	400	425	450
C°	93	107	121	135	149	163	177	191	204	218	232

ABBREVIATIONS

cal = calories   sat = saturated

pro = protein   unsat = unsaturated

g = gram

INTRODUCTION

Welcome to *The Smart Baking Cookbook,* a delightful assortment of smart muffins, cookies, biscuits, and breads.

If this is your first encounter with my Smart Books, get ready for some lovely happenings. You are about to learn what you can do in the kitchen to help your loved ones achieve their greatest potential.

With this book as your guide, you will learn how to provide aromatic baked goods that not only make your taste buds happy, but foster vitality, beautiful complexions, good teeth, pleasant dispositions, and the ability to cope.

But, please, make your moves for more nutritious baked goods when your family isn't looking.

I confess—I am a sneaky cook. I approach each session in the kitchen with a nutritional leer on my mug and a jar of wheat germ behind my back.

You know why? Because I found out early in my overzealous career that with children and with husbands, at various stages in their development—from toddler right up to the coronary stage—anything that smacks of health is not welcomed with shouts of joy. You can't lecture them on the superior merits of your baked goods, and you can't force them. But you can sneak it.

Throughout the various stages of raising four kids from diapers to dungarees, college degrees, Ph.D.s and M.D.s, I have developed a whole big bag of sneaky stratagems. I'll be sharing them with you in many of the recipes that follow.

For starters, just offer every platter of smart muffins, cookies, biscuits, and breads with a big smile; you'll be delighting their taste buds and making them healthy when they're not looking!

SMART INGREDIENTS

FLOURS, GRAINS, AND SEEDS
THAT LENGTHEN YOUR LEASE ON LIFE!

Amaranth

This ancient food of the Aztecs is now available in many natural foods stores. It has many of the cooking properties of grains, but because it is a plant food, not a grain, it can be tolerated by those who are allergic to the wheat family.

Bran

Coarse miller's bran is an excellent source of fiber, which has been shown to prevent many digestive and colon problems. It has a bland flavor, which is not detectable in, for example, cookies, but its dryness causes thirst—and this may encourage the children to drink more milk or juice.

Bran absorbs eight times its volume in water. Be sure to increase your liquid intake when you add bran to your diet.

Like wheat germ, bran should be refrigerated or kept in the freezer. It can be used directly from the freezer.

Cornmeal

Commercially available cornmeal has been stripped of many nutrients as well as the amino acids tryptophan and lysine. Look for stone-ground or water-ground cornmeal. They have undergone much less processing. Their nutritional value and flavor are far superior. Bolted cornmeal has undergone only a rather crude sifting to remove hulls, a process that slightly lowers fiber and calcium content but does not affect other nutrients.

Hi-Lysine Cornmeal

My first choice is Hi-lysine cornmeal derived from a recently developed breed of corn containing high levels of amino acids, especially tryptophan and lysine. Besides providing the necessary amino acids in the proportions in which the body uses them, Hi-lysine cornmeal is organically grown and ground from the whole kernel, including the hull for extra fiber. It is now available at many health food stores, or you can order it from E and D Grain Co., Fullerton, Nebraska 68638.

Millet Flour

Millet flour is ground from millet seed, a grain so rich in minerals that, unlike other grains, it is alkaline-forming rather than acid-forming, making it a perfect addition to the diets of ulcer and colitis patients. Millet is high in protein and B vitamins and is, in fact, the most nutritious of the grain family—and the most neglected. It is a major food source for the long-lived Hunza people of the Himalayas and the taller, stronger natives of northern China. Yet in the United States it has been dubbed "the poor man's cereal" and is mainly used and considered for the birds.

Oat Bran

Oat bran, which has been enjoying considerable popularity recently as a cholesterol-lowering food, is rich in water-soluble fiber. Unlike the insoluble fiber found in wheat bran, which helps speed food through the intestinal tract, soluble fiber delays transit time through the small intestine, where it absorbs cholesterol before it gets into the bloodstream.

Research indicates that oat bran significantly lowers both cholesterol and LDL, the harmful stuff that contributes to hardening of the arteries. Dr. James Anderson, a pioneer in oat bran research at the University of Kentucky College of Medicine, recommends a minimum of 6 grams and a maximum of 10 grams of soluble fiber per day to lower serum cholesterol. A 1-ounce serving of oat bran (about ⅓ cup) provides about 3 grams of soluble fiber.

Does that mean you have to eat two or three bowls of oat bran cereal every day? Not at all. There are many tasty ways to use oat bran. Add it to hot and cold cereals, to pancake and waffle batters. Bake it in muffins and cookies. It's a wonderful thickening agent for soups. Many of my recipes call for at least 2 tablespoons of oat bran.

Don't make the mistake of thinking that just because you're eating oat bran you can overindulge in the bad stuff. Oat bran is most effective when consumed in conjunction with a low-fat, low-cholesterol, high-fiber diet.

Oats

Oat is one grain that somehow manages to survive the refining process with most of its nutrients intact. Rolled oats is simply the generic name for ordinary, commercially available cereal oats or oatmeal. I prefer the nutty flavor of the old-fashioned kind over the instant. Oats are a good source of B vitamins, calcium, potassium, and protein, and contain very little sodium. A little more than 1 cup of oats whizzed in blender or seed mill will give you a cup of oat flour.

Popcorn Flour

Popcorn flour is not available commercially. You make it yourself from freshly popped corn, with no fat or salt added. It takes about 1¼ cups of popped corn to make 1 cup of flour. Grind the popped corn in a blender or seed mill. It contributes a pleasant, corn flavor. Its most attractive asset is its low calorie content—only 50 calories in a cup, as compared to 400 calories in a cup of wheat flour. It is so light and airy, however, that it cannot be used without the support of heavier flours.

Rice Bran

Rice bran is the outside layer of the rice kernel, the part that is removed from brown rice to make white rice. It is rich in protein and an excellent source of the B vitamins, especially thiamine, the "morale vitamin" and an aid to cell growth and development, and niacin, a cholesterol fighter. But that's not all. It's also a veritable gold mine of minerals, providing goodly amounts of calcium, iron, copper, magnesium, and zinc. Because it has no gluten, it can be safely consumed by those who are allergic to most grains.

Rice bran has a nutty-brown color. It has a finer texture and sweeter flavor than oat bran. You can add it to hot and cold breakfast cereals, beverages, and baked goods for more fiber and the glow of health.

Rice bran is the new "kernel" in the army of cholesterol fighters—and may surpass them all in effectiveness. New research conducted by scientists at the U.S. Department of Agriculture reveals that rice bran can lower blood cholesterol levels as well as or better than oat bran.

Rice Flour

Rice flour is made from brown rice and is a good source of iron, protein, minerals, and the B vitamins. Because it is so low in sodium, it is frequently recommended for salt-free diets. It can be used as a substitute for wheat flour for those allergic to wheat.

Seeds

When you stop to think about it, the seed is the very core of life. Its tiny kernel contains a mysterious and fantastic concentration of energy and nutrients designed by Nature, the master chemist, to get the plant up and keep it growing. This core of life in seeds brings vitality to those who consume them.

Consider the powerhouse of nutrients you get in seeds. They are a remarkable, unspoiled source of unsaturated fatty acids. Sunflower seeds are especially high in precious linoleic acid, which helps to prevent harmful deposits of cholesterol and improves resistance to disease by strengthening connective tissue in the cells.

All seeds are rich in nutrients. Pumpkin seeds are 30 percent protein, and high in iron, calcium, phosphorus, and zinc. Sesame seeds are 45 percent protein, and rich in polyunsaturates that are so good for the heart and blood vessels.

Seeds are also rich in vitamin E, which helps maintain normal viscosity in the blood, thus lessening the risk of life-threatening blood clots. They also contain high amounts of the B vitamins—more than you get, in fact, in an equivalent quantity of wheat germ. They are an excellent source of minerals, including the important trace minerals.

One of the most valuable contributions of seeds is their store of enzymes, which initiate and fulfill all vital processes in the cells. Enzymes are as fragile as they are vital, and cooking destroys many of them. Therefore, many of the recipes call for seeds as a garnish, unexposed to heat, so you can reap full value from their life-enhancing nutrients.

A seed mill is a very useful piece of equipment for grinding seeds into meal. It can also be used to grind nuts and pulverize dried orange and lemon peel into powdered rind. It handles small quantities very efficiently. You'll find them at specialty shops and in some health food stores. A coffee grinder can be used instead, if you prefer.

Soy Flour

Soy flour is made from ground soy beans. It is very high in protein (about 40 percent), and remarkably high in potassium (one cup contains 1,636 milligrams). It is available with varying degrees of the original fat left in, as full fat, low fat, and defatted. Since the fat is a good source of lecithin, a substance that emulsifies cholesterol, I use the full-fat variety. It has a strong, almost bitter flavor, and should therefore be used sparingly.

Soy grits and soy flakes are also used in some of the recipes. Soy grits are coarsely ground soy beans, not subjected to heat, and soy flakes are derived from lightly toasted beans that have been flaked. They have the nutritional qualities of soy beans but cook up much faster.

Soy, the great protein booster, has twice as much protein as wheat flour and lots more potassium, calcium, iron, and B-complex vitamins.

The amino acids of soy complement those of wheat. (Soy is high in lysine, low in methionine. Wheat is just the opposite.) Together they provide all the essential amino acids in proportions that are most efficiently utilized by the body.

It takes only 2 tablespoons of soy flour at the bottom of a cup of wheat flour to greatly enhance the protein, mineral, and vitamin values of your smart recipes.

Wheat Bran

Bran is the outer coating of the wheat berry, which is removed in the refining process. Bran is a good source of the B vitamins and minerals and an excellent source of fiber. Stripped from the wheat, bran is an aid to the digestive system and has been shown to provide protection against polyps and diseases of the colon. It also protects against gallbladder disease, and it decreases the absorption of cholesterol and unfriendly fats, significantly reducing the incidence of cardiovascular disease.

Wheat Germ

There are some foods which, when used liberally, provide you with a broad spectrum of almost all the vitamins, minerals, and enzymes you need to keep that wonderful machine of yours in tip-top shape. It's unfortunate that one of these foods should have an unattractive name—making it sound like something that creeps! In this instance, however, the word "germ" means heart or essence of life; wheat germ is rich in life-giving nutrients that made bread the staff of life before flour was refined.

Unless you are using whole wheat flour, the wheat germ has been removed from the flour in your canister. It's been removed from most commercial baked goods—bread, cakes, crackers, noodles, and cookies. Why? Because wheat germ supports life; it attracts life-seeking insects and spoils more readily. Without the life-enhancing wheat germ, flour has a longer shelf life and can be shipped all over the world. It is therefore commercially expedient to remove the wheat germ from the flour.

What about enriched flour? That word "enriched" has been pulling the wool over our eyes and leading us down the path to deficiency diseases for too many years.

In the so-called enrichment process, only three or four of the thirty-three nutrients in wheat germ are put back in the flour, in only one third of the original amount, and in a synthetic form, which your body does not use effectively. Inorganic iron, for example, interferes with the body's use of vitamin E.

Wheat germ provides a bonanza of nutrients: lots of protein to repair and build cells, tissues, and organs; polyunsaturated oil for glowing complexions and efficient metabolism; vitamin E to protect polyunsaturates from oxidation, thus retarding the aging process and damage to the circulatory system; and practically every member of the B-complex family, in generous amounts. These vitamins are crucial to maintaining a healthy heart, an upbeat attitude, and a clear-thinking mind. Some of the B vitamins have been shown to improve the developing intelligence of young children.

Wheat germ also provides a veritable gold mine of minerals—magnesium, potassium, and calcium, essential to every beat of the heart; and zinc, so important to growth in children, to one's sense of taste and smell, to the ability to heal, to a blemish-free complexion, and to fertility and the health of the prostate gland.

Either toasted or raw wheat germ can be used in these recipes. Raw wheat germ has slightly more nutritional value; the toasted has better keeping qualities and a flavor more acceptable to some palates. I suggest using raw wheat germ in recipes that require baking and toasted wheat germ in unbaked confections.

Keep wheat germ in the refrigerator, or, better yet, in the freezer. It can be used directly from the freezer and will stay fresh longer. Never use rancid wheat germ. If you have a jar that's been around for more than a month, give it the sniff-and-taste test. If it has an off odor or leaves a bitter aftertaste, discard it and get a fresh supply.

Whole Wheat Flour

Regular whole wheat flour used in bread-making is ground from hard winter wheat and contains a high degree of gluten. Gluten gives the flour the ability to absorb more liquid, which helps the dough to rise. Whole wheat pastry flour, the kind recommended for Smart Baking recipes, contributes to a finer texture. Both kinds contain many life-enhancing nutrients.

Because smart recipes call for smart ingredients, I avoid white flour, since it has been emasculated in the refining process. Instead, I use whole wheat flour almost exclusively. The recipes for the allergic call for other types of whole grain flours.

FAT

Fat—it's not all bad. Fat provides energy, insulates the body against temperature changes, and helps you utilize the fat-soluble vitamins—A, D, E, and K—which function in tandem with other vitamins and minerals. So don't cut fats out of your diet completely, even if you're overweight.

The trouble is, most Americans get too much fat. High-fat diets have been linked to increased levels of cardiovascular disease and cancer of the breast and colon.

Many health professionals feel we would be wise to cut our fat intake to 20 percent of total calories. At present the American Heart Association's Dietary Goals suggest that no more than 30 percent of calories come from fat and that no more than 10 percent of that 30 percent should be *saturated* fat.

It's the saturated fats that lead to increased levels of serum cholesterol. In nature, they are found mostly in dairy products, meat, lard, and other animal products. You can cut down on them by eating fewer meat products, by using dairy products that are chiefly low fat and nonfat, and, if you love butter, by using Healthy Heart Butter (page 14).

But there are other, less obvious culprits. Margarines, solid shortenings, processed cheeses, hydrogenated peanut butter, and packaged cake mixes, along with many other processed foods, contain saturated fats as well.

Other sources of hidden saturated fats are the tropical oils of coconut, palm, and palm kernel. They are more highly saturated than meat. They are used in many foods—margarines, coffee creamers, dessert toppings, chocolates, cereals, many processed foods, and even infant formulas. When a label says "pure vegetable oil" without specifying which oil, it could be one of these tropical oils. Food manufacturers, now aware of the problem, are in the process of switching. So *read the labels*.

The American Heart Association and the National Cancer Institute both recommend a diet containing no more than 30 percent of calories from fat, with equal amounts of all three types: 10 percent polyunsaturates, 10 percent monounsaturates, and 10 percent saturated fats (butter, beef fat, coconut oil, and palm oil).

Polyunsaturates

Safflower, sunflower, soy, and corn oil are polyunsaturated oils providing essential fatty acids, important building blocks for every cell in the body. They are called essential because the body cannot manufacture them—they must be consumed. Polyunsaturates have another function: They lower the LDL (low-density lipoprotein) content of cholesterol, a maneuver that contributes to cardiovascular health. LDLs are the bad guys in the cholesterol family. They contribute to the formation of artery-clogging clots. However, polyunsaturates also tend to lower HDL (high-density lipoproteins), which tend to protect the arteries by preventing formation of clots.

Polyunsaturates are also chemically very reactive, meaning they are converted by oxygen into peroxides, which break down into free radicals that damage the cells of the body, causing a predisposition to aging and malignancies. Nature, in her infinite wisdom, packages these fatty acids with vitamin E, an antioxidant. It prevents peroxidation, but processing removes the vitamin E. It is therefore important to supplement

12

your intake of polyunsaturated oils with vitamin E, both internally and externally—that is, besides the vitamin E you take as a supplement, protect the oils in your salad dressing by squeezing the contents of a 400 I.U. vitamin E capsule in each pint of polyunsaturated oil.

Monounsaturates

Olive oil and peanut oil are monounsaturates. Sesame oil is very close to being a monounsaturate.

One of the most exciting developments in nutrition is our new understanding of the role of dietary fats in the pursuit and maintenance of health. For some time it was thought that monounsaturates were neutral, that they neither lowered nor raised cholesterol levels. But a study by Fred Mattson, Ph.D., of the University of California at San Diego, reveals that monounsaturates are *cholesterol reducers* just as effective as the polyunsaturates. However, whereas both types of fat reduce the LDL fraction, the monounsaturates do not (as the polyunsaturates do) lower the HDL, and in some instances the monounsaturates actually raise the HDL. The ability of the monounsaturates to lower the bad fraction and increase the good fraction makes them an even better friend of the cardiovascular system than the polyunsaturates. Also, the monounsaturates are more stable than the polyunsaturates, less subject to peroxidation or rancidity, and more stable when exposed to heat. For this reason, the monounsaturates are preferable for cooking and baking.

Butter

Pure unsalted, sweet butter is the kind that goes into smart recipes—but the amount is greatly reduced. The trouble with butter is its saturated fat content. By law, butter must be 80 percent milkfat. As much as

65 percent of that fat is saturated. In small amounts, though, butter provides so much salivary pleasure that its benefits exceed its risks.

Do not be tempted to substitute margarine for butter. There is no comparison in taste and healthwise you're much better off with butter. The hydrogenation process converts the polyunsaturated fatty acids into trans-fatty acids, which are more damaging to the arteries than saturated fats or cholesterol.

Butter has the same number of calories as margarine, and 20 percent fewer calories than oil.

Oil is 100 percent fat, while butter is 20 percent water and 80 percent fat. If you wish to substitute oil for butter, use 20 percent less oil. For example, if the recipe calls for 1 cup of butter, use 1 cup of oil minus 3 tablespoons, and add 3 tablespoons of liquid to the recipe. If the recipe does not call for any liquid, add 3 tablespoons of water or fruit juice with the oil.

Healthy Heart Butter has half the saturated-fat content and, instead, is combined with beneficial mono- and polyunsaturated oils.

Healthy Heart Butter

This polyunsaturated butter banishes the fear of butter. It has an excellent country-fresh flavor and is rich in essential fatty acids. It has 4 times as much polyunsaturated fat as saturated. Since only 2 grams of polyunsaturated fat neutralizes the cholesterol-raising effect of 1 gram of saturated fat, this butter is a polyunsaturated wonder. The linseed oil that is blended with the butter is extremely rich in linoleic acid, which reduces the tendency of blood platelets to clump together and form clots in the arteries. Olive oil, which contributes 10 grams of monounsaturates, has been shown to reduce harmful cholesterol. But just because Healthy

Heart Butter is better for you doesn't mean you should slather it on indiscriminately. All fats are high in calories and should be consumed in moderation.

½ cup (1 stick) unsalted butter, cut in 8 pieces

¼ cup linseed oil (cold pressed), food quality

2 tablespoons safflower or sunflower oil

1 tablespoon olive oil

Combine all ingredients in a blender or food processor and whiz for 2 minutes or until all ingredients are blended together. Mold into 2 small bowls and store in the freezer. May be used directly from the freezer. Use for spreading. For baking and sautéing, substitute olive or canola oil for the linseed oil.

Yield: Makes 1 cup.

1 tablespoon provides: 104 cal, 5.7 g sat fat, 22.7 g unsat fat.

Variation 1:

To further increase the cholesterol-lowering potential of Healthy Heart Butter, add 2 tablespoons of lecithin granules to the ingredients and then process in the food processor or blender. Use this version for the table and for baking, or for sautéing.

Variation 2:

For Healthy Heart Butter to be used on pancakes, or waffles, or for baking muffins, add 1 to 2 tablespoons grated orange rind to the ingredients before processing.

Variation 3:

Instead of olive oil, use any of the following, which, according to *Controlling Cholesterol* (Bantam, 1988) by Kenneth H. Cooper, M.D., contribute the same amount of monounsaturates as 1 tablespoon of olive oil: 1½ tablespoons almond butter or 3½ tablespoons almonds; 2½ tablespoons peanut butter or ¼ cup peanuts; 3 tablespoons hazelnuts; 3½ tablespoons pecans; ¼ cup pistachios; 4 teaspoons canola oil (an unflavored mono oil made from rapeseed).

Variation 4:
To reduce the calories in Healthy Heart Butter, blend together 1 stick of butter, ¼ cup linseed oil, and ¼ cup yogurt or buttermilk. Use as a spread. *Only 84 calories in a tablespoon.*

Cholesterol

There is increasing evidence that elevated cholesterol is associated with increased risk of heart disease. The consensus is that for every 1 percent that you lower your serum cholesterol, you will decrease your risk of dying from a heart attack by 2 percent.

A cholesterol level of 200 or lower is classified as "desirable" by the National Heart, Lung, and Blood Institute. From 200 to 239 is "borderline"; from 240 to 260, "moderate risk"; and beyond that "high risk."

When the ratio of a person's total blood cholesterol to HDL is 5:1, that individual has a normal risk of heart disease. When the total cholesterol to HDL ratio is 8:1, there is twice the risk, and when the ratio is 4:1, only half the normal risk.

Let's say you have a total cholesterol of 240 and an HDL of 60. Congratulations: Your ratio is 4:1. You have only half the normal risk of heart disease. Suppose your total cholesterol is 240 and your HDL is only 30. Your ratio is 8:1, or twice the risk. Stock up on beans, oat bran, lecithin granules, olive or canola oil, fruits, vegetables, nuts, and seeds. These are the foods that have been shown to lower total cholesterol and improve HDL levels.

Now let's look at your LDL, which is a more certain indicator of cholesterol risk. If LDL is above 160, the situation is defined as high risk. If the LDL is from 130 to 159, the situation needs attention but the risk is not as great. You can reduce your LDL by cutting back on saturated fats and by eliminating caffeine, sugar, white flour, cigarettes, and alcohol. Increase your consumption of the foods listed above that raise HDL levels.

If you have an elevated cholesterol, it does not necessarily mean that you are consuming too much cholesterol. Your elevated cholesterol may be the result of total dietary fat consumed—especially the saturated type—and may come from eating excessive animal protein, insufficient fiber, too much sugar, and from imbalances of vitamins or minerals. Or it can be the result of a lack of exercise or of being overweight. Or it could be from emotional stress.

Edward R. Pinckney, M.D., points out that cholesterol levels increase in response to some emotional situations. In one series of experiments, the cholesterol levels of medical students shot up immediately after an examination was announced. Soldiers have shown elevated cholesterol levels when required to perform a dangerous mission.

But don't let "cholesterol mania" take the joy out of eating! Remember that some cholesterol is necessary, even beneficial. The body uses it as a major constituent of cell membranes. It is an essential component of most body tissues, especially those of the brain and nervous system. It is needed to form sex and adrenal hormones, vitamin D, and bile, which is needed for the digestion of fats.

Good and Bad Cholesterol

Those people who have the lowest incidence of heart disease are those who have very high levels of HDL (high-density lipoprotein). This is the "good" cholesterol, which acts like a vacuum cleaner, sweeping through the bloodstream, picking up cholesterol and facilitating its elimination from the body through its conversion to bile.

The "bad" cholesterols are the LDLs, and to some extent the VLDLs (low-density and very low-density lipoproteins). They work their mischief by depositing fatty materials on the arterial walls while the HDLs prevent cholesterol from being deposited and hasten its removal.

SWEETENERS

The sweeteners used in most commercial baking are refined sugar, either white or brown (white sugar with a little molasses added for color), and corn syrup, which is also highly refined and depleted of nutrients. These refined sweeteners make a mad rush for the bloodstream without paying a courtesy call on the liver, whose job it is to dole out the sugar in usable amounts. An abundance of sugar in the bloodstream triggers an overproduction of insulin, which transports the sugar out of the blood and into the cells of the body, where it is converted into fat (making it very hard to zip your jeans).

In its eagerness to do its job, insulin overreacts and reduces the blood sugar to dangerously low levels. This causes hypoglycemia (low blood sugar), a condition that can masquerade as mental disorders, fatigue, temper tantrums, or erratic behavior. We agonize over "what's eating the kids" when they are irritable. Perhaps it's time to start wondering what the kids have been eating!

A recent landmark study conducted at the Tidewater Detention Homes in Tidewater, Virginia, revealed that by revising the diets of 276 juveniles, antisocial behavior declined by 44 percent, there were 77 percent fewer incidents of theft, 82 percent fewer incidents of assault, and a 55 percent reduction in the refusal to obey orders. What brought about

18

this remarkable improvement in deportment? The amount of sugar in the young people's diets had been considerably reduced.

There is no refined sugar or corn syrup in these smart recipes. Indeed, all sweetening agents have been reduced to a bare minimum because no sweetener should be used in excessive amounts. You'll be able to detect the lovely natural sweetness that is present in all wholesome food.

The following sweeteners contain some vitamins, minerals, and enzymes, which means they do not rush to your bloodstream and do not deplete your body's supply of vitamins in order to be metabolized.

Barley Malt Syrup

Barley malt syrup is a grain sweetener made from malted or germinated barley. It is 65 percent maltose and has much less sweetening power than sugar or honey, but since it does not need insulin for metabolizing, it does not trigger fluctuations in blood sugar levels.

Frozen Fruit Juice Concentrates

Fruit juice concentrates are incredibly sweet and rich in nutrients and can be substituted for or used in conjunction with other sweeteners. The fruits they are derived from may vary in sweetness, so give your batter the taste test. You may need a little more of another sweetener for the most appealing flavor.

Honey

Honey is twice as sweet as sugar, so you can use half as much to achieve the same level of sweetness. Honey has other advantages over sugar. Honey's sweetness is derived mainly from fructose, which, unlike sucrose, does not trigger an outpouring of insulin. Fructose is also absorbed into the bloodstream at a much slower rate. It is, therefore, less likely to cause the "sugar blues."

Nutritionally, honey provides B vitamins and small amounts of important minerals like calcium, phosphorus, iron, and potassium, as well as certain enzymes. By contrast, sugar contains no nutrients whatsoever.

Honey should be used raw, unfiltered, and unprocessed. For the least processed honey, you'd have to visit the keeper of the bees! Next best, and more practical, is your health food store. If the honey in your jar has crystallized, rejoice! That's a sign that it has not been damaged by excessive heat. Just put the jar in warm water for a few minutes and the honey will liquefy.

Clover honey is the mildest in flavor and is recommended for baked goods while you are weaning the family away from sugar. Once they are accustomed to the taste of honey, try other varieties. Buckwheat, my favorite, tastes great in muffins if you want the flavor of honey to dominate.

When converting old recipes that call for sugar, use ½ cup honey for every cup of sugar. Reduce the liquid in the recipe by ½ cup for every cup of honey and bake at a temperature 25°F lower than the instructions call for. If there is no liquid in the recipe, add ¼ cup more flour. (There is no need to make these adjustments for the recipes in this book.)

Maple Syrup

Maple syrup contains 65 percent sucrose, as compared to sugar cane and turbinado sugar, both of which are almost 100 percent sucrose. Brown sugar is about 96 percent sucrose. Sucrose is the culprit that triggers the fluctuations in the blood sugar levels mentioned earlier that result in depression and exhaustion.

Look for pure, 100 percent maple syrup. Avoid the maple-flavored syrups, which may contain as little as 2 percent maple syrup and that are in reality 95 percent sucrose.

Maple Syrup Granules

Maple syrup granules are a dry, all-natural sweetener made from pure maple syrup. In the conversion from syrup to powder, nothing is added and nothing is removed except water. It needs no refrigeration and will not ferment. The granules, tiny beige pellets, can be reconstituted by adding boiling water or can be used as a dry sweetener to replace cane sugar. Rich in calcium, they have much less sodium than honey.

Molasses

Unsulphured molasses is made from the juice of sugar cane. One tablespoon of first extraction or light molasses provides 33 milligrams of calcium, 183 milligrams of potassium, and almost 1 milligram of iron.

One tablespoon of second extraction or medium molasses provides 137 milligrams of calcium (as much as half a glass of milk), 213 milligrams of potassium, and 1.2 milligrams of iron.

One tablespoon of third extraction or blackstrap molasses provides 137 milligrams of calcium, 585 milligrams of potassium (more than you get in two oranges), and 3.2 milligrams of iron (that's ten times as much iron as you would get in a tablespoon of raisins), and only 43 calories. For that same 43 calories, you also get an extra bonus of magnesium, zinc, copper, chromium, and small amounts of thiamine, riboflavin, and niacin.

The flavor of blackstrap is strong and pervasive, and it has only half the sweetening power of sugar. For best results, it's a good idea to use honey or some other sweetener in conjunction with grain sweeteners and molasses, so that one flavor does not predominate.

Rice and Sorghum Syrups

Rice and sorghum syrups are also derived from grains and can be used to increase both moistness and the keeping quality of your cookies. Sorghum tastes very much like molasses.

OTHER INGREDIENTS

Baking Powder

Look for a brand of baking powder that is aluminum-free. Royal Baking Powder is a good commercial brand without aluminum. Cellu, another brand available at most health food stores, is both aluminum- and sodium-free.

You can make your own baking powder by combining ¼ teaspoon of baking soda with ½ teaspoon of cream of tartar. This is equivalent to 1 teaspoon of baking powder. To make a larger supply, combine 1 tablespoon of baking soda, 2 tablespoons of cream of tartar, and 2 tablespoons of arrowroot powder. The arrowroot protects the other two ingredients from absorbing moisture and reacting to each other. Seal tightly and store in a cool, dry place. Makes ¼ cup.

Carob

Carob powder is derived from the fruit of the carob tree. The carob pods are dried, seeded, and skinned. In ancient times, the seed of the carob pod was used as the standard for the weight of the carat, still used as the standard for the measurement of precious metals and jewels. Carob is also known as St. John's bread. Legend has it that St. John survived on the fruit of the carob tree while he was in the desert. It is also known in Yiddish as *boeksur* (pronounced "buck-tzer") and is distributed to Jewish children on the holiday Tu B'Shevat, which celebrates the life-giving quality of the carob tree. It tastes like chocolate.

Unlike chocolate, however, carob contains natural sweeteners, and therefore requires fewer added sweeteners and is far less caloric. Three and a half ounces of bittersweet chocolate contain 477 calories, 39.7 grams of fat, and 1.8 grams of fiber; the equivalent amount of carob contains 180 calories, 1.4 grams of fat, and a whopping 7.7 grams of roughage—which puts carob in the same league as wheat bran in the fiber department. Its carbohydrates are derived from fruit sugars, which have a low fat content—2 percent in carob compared to 52 percent in chocolate. The pectin content of carob has proved valuable in the treatment of diarrhea.

If your family is unaccustomed to the slightly different taste and aroma of carob, adding a tablespoon or two of cocoa to the carob container will make the whole thing taste like cocoa.

Grated Orange Rind

Many of the recipes call for grated orange rind, not only for its flavor, but also for its many important nutrients—vitamin C, vitamin A, calcium, trace minerals, and the important bioflavonoids, which strengthen cartilage, preventing varicose veins, bleeding gums, and a host of other ailments.

Here's how to have an endless supply: Every time you use an orange, wash it thoroughly with a stiff brush, then dry it. Using a vegetable peeler, peel off the orange layer of skin. Wrap this skin in paper toweling and place it in a warm place to dry. When it is dry and brittle, store it in a jar. When a recipe calls for orange rind, put a handful of these dried rinds in your seed mill, coffee grinder, or blender. You'll have lovely fresh-ground orange rind with an enticing aroma and flavor.

Lecithin

Lecithin is another marvelous, life-enhancing substance. Recent research done in Israel revealed that as little as 1 tablespoon of lecithin granules daily was able to lower LDL cholesterol levels and triglycerides significantly. It also reduced plaque formation in the bloodstream. That alone should be enough to make you reach for the lecithin granules, but there's more. Lecithin can keep you on your toes mentally. M.I.T. scientists have shown that lecithin in the diet improves memory and actually makes one "smarter." It does this by helping the body to manufacture acetylcholine, a substance that helps the brain to transmit nerve signals. Soybeans and eggs are both good sources of lecithin.

Lecithin is a fatty substance that acts as a natural emulsifier and helps keep your blood's cholesterol circulating freely. Research indicates that lecithin increases by a factor of three the amount of cholesterol dissolved in bile salts, the vehicle by which the body rids itself of excess cholesterol.

Nutritional or Brewer's Yeast

Nutritional yeast, also known as brewer's yeast, should not be confused with baker's yeast, which is used to raise dough. Brewer's yeast is a food supplement, a concentrated source of B vitamins, minerals, and high-quality protein—all this and no fat. Studies have shown that only one tablespoon of brewer's yeast a day can reduce cholesterol levels, raise glucose tolerance, and increase the ability to handle stress. Add a little to all your baked goods, and you'll easily down a tablespoon daily.

SUBSTITUTIONS FOR INTOLERANCES

Making substitutions based on these guidelines will permit you to make with success any recipe in this book.

Gluten Intolerance

Gluten is the protein in wheat that combines with yeast to make bread rise. Barley, oats, rye, and triticale also contain gluten but in lesser amounts than wheat. Hard wheat has more gluten than the soft wheat from which pastry flour is made. It is important to know that the most nutritious parts of the wheat, the wheat germ and the bran, have no gluten, and you can enjoy them in good health. Other grains that are gluten-free are corn, millet, rice, amaranth, buckwheat, and quinoa.

Wheat Intolerance

If you are allergic to wheat, you can use other grains like barley, rye, millet, rice, oats, amaranth, and buckwheat. Don't be confused by the name buckwheat. It is not related to wheat, not even a second cousin twice removed. Buckwheat is a member of the rhubarb family and is a very wholesome grain, rich in rutin, a bioflavonoid that strengthens cartilage.

Consider these substitutions for 1 cup of wheat flour:

> 1⅓ cups ground rolled oats;
> or ⅝ cup rice flour plus ⅓ cup rye flour;
> or ½ cup barley flour;
> or 1¼ cups rye flour

Milk Intolerance

If you are allergic to milk, use herbal tea or fruit juice in recipes calling for milk. Or try these delicious nut milks:

Peanut Milk: Blend together ½ cup shelled, skinned peanuts with 2 cups of water. Strain. The chunks that remain can be added to granola or baked goods, or noshed on the spot.

Almond Milk: Blend together ½ cup almonds with 1 to 2 cups of water. Add small amounts of water at a time until achieving the desired consistency.

Sesame Milk: Blend ½ cup sesame seeds with ½ cup water, then add another cup of water, more or less depending on the consistency you prefer. Use less water when you want a substitute for cream.

Soy Milk: Combine 1 cup soy powder with 3 cups water in a large saucepan. Whisk until well dissolved. Bring to the boil over high heat, stirring constantly. Lower heat and simmer for 3 minutes. Serve hot or cold.

Many people who are lactose-intolerant can handle yogurt. While they lack lactase, the enzyme needed to digest the lactose in the milk, the fermentation process, which converts milk to yogurt, converts the lactose to lactic acid.

To make up for a lack of calcium, try these tips:

- Use blackstrap molasses as the sweetener in all baked goods, puddings, and confections. One tablespoon of blackstrap molasses provides 137 milligrams of calcium.
- Always use carob instead of chocolate. There is four times as much calcium in carob as there is in cocoa.
- An excellent source of calcium is sesame seeds—the brown ones with their hulls on. One hundred grams or slightly less than ¼ pound contains a whopping 1,160 milligrams of calcium. When they are hulled, they contain 100 milligrams of calcium.
- Look for tahini made from unhulled sesame seeds or make your own by grinding sesame seeds in a little seed mill or coffee grinder. Add a tiny bit of sesame oil to get peanut butter consistency.
- Add a little lemon juice to tahini—diluted with water—and it makes a great salad dressing.
- Combine tahini with ground coconut, sunflower seeds, and wheat germ. Add a bit of honey and blackstrap molasses and you have a dynamite confection—halvah.

Sour milk may be used as a substitute for buttermilk or yogurt. To make sour milk, simply add 2 teaspoons of lemon juice or vinegar to a cup of milk.

Corn Intolerance

If you're allergic to corn and a recipe calls for cornstarch, substitute whole wheat flour, soy flour, brown rice flour, potato starch, or arrow-root starch. Most baking powders include cornstarch. Make your own corn-free baking powder by combining ¼ teaspoon bicarbonate of soda with ½ teaspoon cream of tartar. This is equivalent to 1 teaspoon baking powder. If you are on a strict salt-free diet, use potassium bicarbonate (available at most pharmacies) instead of sodium bicarbonate.

Egg Intolerance

If you're allergic to eggs, it may be just the white that is bothering you. In that case you can still enjoy the yolks.

Duck eggs can sometimes be handled by those allergic to hen eggs.

Whether it's just the albumin or the whole egg you can't handle, re-member that commercial egg substitutes are not egg-free. They contain egg whites and nonfat milk solids. (Also, make sure you're not given any vaccines produced in eggs. Vaccines for measles, mumps, rubella, and influenza are usually made with eggs.)

BAKE YOUR OWN BREAD

Fill the house with that wonderful yeasty fragrance of home-made bread. There is no accomplishment more satisfying and no aroma more wonderful to come home to.

If you have never baked a loaf of bread, you have missed out on one of life's most elemental joys. Nothing gives me more pleasure than watching my family enjoy a loaf of bread that I have magically conjured up, with the help of my oven, out of a little yeast, flour, eggs, and maybe a little oil.

I love seeing my children share in the same excitement and wonder that I experienced when I watched my mother bake. She would sing as she mixed and kneaded and braided. In my mind there was something magical about the way she filled the house with such a tantalizing, yeasty, appetite-stimulating fragrance, and then produced those beautiful and delicious breads and cakes.

Now that white bread is an everyday empty-calorie commodity, more available than a good, tasty, wholesome whole-grain bread, try using whole wheat flour, or a mixture of whole wheat and unbleached white.

Stone-ground flour is preferable. Keep it in the refrigerator or freezer and buy it from a source where it is kept refrigerated. The regular whole wheat flour that is used in breadmaking is ground from hard winter wheat and contains a high degree of gluten, which helps the dough to rise. When you are baking with yeast, warm the flour to room temperature. Put as much as you need in the oven at 200°F for about 15 minutes or put it in the microwave oven on high for 1 minute.

For quick breads, muffins, and cookies use whole wheat pastry flour, which is ground from soft wheat. It contributes a finer texture.

Both kinds contain the germ and the bran that are removed from white flour and thus provide many life-enhancing nutrients.

If your family is still accustomed to white bread, use only 1 cup of whole wheat flour in your first batch. Gradually replace more of the white with whole wheat. You may never get them to accept a 100 percent whole wheat bread, but don't despair: instead, for every cup of unbleached white flour you use, take away one heaping tablespoon and substitute one heaping tablespoon of wheat germ. Put the wheat germ with some flour in the blender and whiz it fine. This will give the wheat germ a finer texture and will, in effect, sift the flour. Remeasure the flour after blending.

Helpful Hints on Baking a Good Loaf of Bread

Assemble your equipment before you begin: a large mixing bowl, two measuring cups, a rubber spatula. If you have an electric beater, use it to develop the gluten in the flour.

Have all ingredients at room temperature.

When mixing the last portion of the flour into your dough, use only enough to assure a silky but non-sticky dough.

Oil your hands slightly before kneading.

If you use raw potato water in your bread wherever plain water is called for, you have a better chance of getting a bread that does not crumble.

To make raw potato water, put a diced potato in a measuring cup and fill with tepid water. Whiz in blender. If you don't have a blender, grate the potato instead of dicing it. Put pulp in measuring cup, fill with water and mix thoroughly.

Sprouts (wheat, rye, alfalfa) can be added to any bread dough to make a superior, moist, delicious loaf. Sprouts can be chopped, blended, or used whole. Work them into the dough during the last kneading. Limit the sprouts to 1 cup for every 2 cups of liquid in the recipe.

Many of the recipes for baked goods call for greasing the baking utensil with a mixture of oil and liquid lecithin (food quality). This mixture works very well.

However, a baking spray may be more convenient for you.

When spritzing with a baking spray, turn your head away and cover your nose so that you don't inhale the propellant.

Bear in mind that the spray is flammable. Never leave the spray can on the stove, or near heat or an open flame.

NUTRIENT CONTENT OF INGREDIENTS

Almonds Excellent source of protein, potassium, iron, calcium, phosphorus, and essential fatty acids.

Amaranth Not exactly a household word, but fast gaining popularity with American cooks. Amaranth is a plant food valued for its nutritious leaves and seeds, which are higher in protein than grains like wheat and rye. Because it is a plant food and not a grain, it is acceptable to those allergic to wheat or other grains.

Apricots High source of vitamin A, and provides the B vitamin niacin, magnesium, calcium, phosphorus, and iron.

Bananas Good source of potassium, some vitamin A, and vitamin C.

Barley Malt Syrup Provides protein, calcium, and some B vitamins.

Bran The outer coating of the wheat, corn, or rice grain, bran is a particularly good source of niacin, potassium, iron, phosphorus, calcium, and minerals, and it is high in fiber.

Buckwheat Good source of protein, complex carbohydrates, and minerals.

Carob Flour or powder is 8% protein and over 70% carbohydrate, and is an exceptionally good source of calcium and phosphorus.

Cashew Nuts Good source of protein, potassium, phosphorus, calcium, and some iron.

Cheese, Ricotta Sometimes called "Italian cottage cheese," this is higher in fat and calories than cottage cheese. One cup of ricotta made from whole milk contains about 430 calories and 32 grams of fat. When made from part skim milk, it contains 340 calories and 19 grams of fat. A cup of creamed cottage cheese contains only 215 calories and 9 grams of fat.

Coconut Shreds   The meat of the coconut, dried, then shredded. An excellent sweetener that provides calcium, phosphorus, iron, potassium, and small amounts of the B vitamins.

Cornmeal (Hy-Lysine)   Made from corn containing higher levels of amino acids, especially lysine, which is usually low in grains. Most cornmeal is low in protein, but Hi-lysine provides protein of very high biological value, as well as iron, calcium, magnesium, potassium, B vitamins, and vitamin A.

Figs   Good source of potassium and magnesium, and provides some iron and B vitamins.

Honey   Provides some potassium, magnesium, calcium, and traces of the B vitamins.

Lecithin Granules   Derived from soybeans, they contain a rich supply of choline and inositol, which are members of the B-vitamin family and are essential to the production of lecithin and the utilization of fats.

Maple Syrup   A naturally occurring sweetener rich in minerals.

Millet   Provides protein and some B vitamins (especially thiamine).

Molasses, Blackstrap or Third Extraction   Excellent source of iron and calcium.

Oats or Rolled Oats   Provide potassium, calcium, iron, magnesium, zinc, and contribute a pleasant nutty flavor.

Orange Juice Concentrate   Provides potassium, phosphorus, calcium, magnesium, vitamins C and A, and traces of the B vitamins.

Peanut Butter   Crunchy or smooth, it furnishes protein, unsaturated fatty acids, minerals, and the B vitamin niacin.

Pecans Provide protein, unsaturated fatty acids, potassium, calcium, some iron, and traces of the B vitamins.

Pumpkin Seeds A good source of zinc.

Raisins Contain iron, calcium, potassium, magnesium, some vitamin B6, and traces of the other B vitamins.

Rice Flour Made from ground short-grain brown rice, this type of flour provides protein, potassium, magnesium, calcium, the B vitamins (notably niacin), and fiber.

Rice Syrup A sweetener made from brown rice, it provides protein, calcium, vitamins B1 (thiamine) and B2 (riboflavin), and a big dose of iron.

Sesame Seeds Provide unsaturated fatty acids, calcium, magnesium, phosphorus, and small amounts of vitamin A and the B vitamins.

Sorghum Syrup The concentrated juice of sorghum, a cereal grain related to corn; provides a smattering of iron, phosphorus, and calcium.

Soy Flour Made from ground soybeans, it has a high protein content (35%) and is also high in fat (20%). It's available with various degrees of fats removed and its amino acids complement those of wheat. Soy flour has no gluten, making it safe for those who cannot tolerate gluten, but it will not raise the bread.

Sunflower Seeds An excellent snack food, they are a powerhouse of nutrients, including protein, B vitamins, iron, phosphorus, calcium, and a highly digestible polyunsaturated oil.

Tahini Also known as sesame butter, it's rich in important linoleic acid, which helps the body utilize fats.

Tofu Derived from soybeans, and sometimes called soy cheese. A versatile protein food, rich in the B vitamin choline, minerals, and lecithin.

Walnuts Supply a good mix of all the important minerals, as well as vitamin A, the B-vitamin family, and vitamin C; also an excellent source of protein and essential fatty acids.

Wheat Germ The heart of the wheat berry, it's tremendously nutritious—rich in protein, B vitamins, and vitamin E, and many minerals.

Whole Wheat Flour Made from whole wheat berries with germ, bran, and endosperm (the white part) all intact, whole wheat flour is a good source of potassium, iron, vitamin B1 (thiamine), calcium, and protein.

Yeast, Brewer's or Nutritional Excellent source of protein, the B vitamins, and many important minerals.

MAKE YOUR OWN MUFFINS

My love for muffins goes back to my early childhood. Mom baked muffins that reflected her mood and our economic status. She made them with extra raisins when she was very pleased with us, like when we got good report cards or practiced the piano without being told. She threw in extra nuts when Dad's business was booming. Streusel toppings appeared on them when company came. She even made muffins when she was troubled about something she had no control over, like the time my brother was in the hospital with a broken leg. They seemed to pick up her spirits—and my brother's.

I even named my favorite doll "Muffin."

There's something very lovable about muffins. They announce their presence with an enticing aroma, bring smiles to cranky sleepy-heads, recharge your body's batteries, and leave you with a sparkle in your eyes and a wonderful taste in your mouth. They're a cinch to make, too, and don't make a big dent in your grocery bill.

Muffins are certainly a delightful way to start the day, but they're not just for breakfast. Their many merits have won them top status as a convenience food that goes to school for lunch, to the office for coffee breaks, into backpacks for nourishment on the trail, and into your handbag for morale-boosting sustenance on the bus, train, or plane. Best of all, they provide a delicious solution to that perpetual question, "What's to eat, Mom?"

But if you, like me, have an urge to see the glow of health on the faces of your loved ones, you will make all your muffins Smart Muffins.

Smart Muffins, like Smart Cookies, do not expand your waistline with empty calories. They don't clog your arteries with lots of fat. Smart Muffins are high in fiber; ridiculously low in fat; and contain no sugar, salt, white flour, hydrogenated fats, or chemical additives. They're rich in nutrients that strengthen bones, like calcium, magnesium, and zinc; nutrients that help you handle stress, like pantothenic acid, a B vitamin that is lost in the refining process; nutrients that contribute to a pleasant disposition like B_1, called the "morale vitamin"; and nutrients that increase vitality, growth, and stamina, like zinc and vitamin E.

California psychiatrist Michael Lesser, in his address before the U.S. Senate Select Committee on Nutrition and Human Needs, quoted the great twelfth-century physician Moses Maimonides:

"No illness which can be treated by diet should be treated by any other means."

I'm not suggesting that you should treat your illnesses with Smart Muffins. I am suggesting that Smart Muffins in your daily diet provide you with many nutrients that can prevent illness. And as everybody knows, an ounce of prevention is worth a pound of cure.

Just because these muffins are smart doesn't mean they're boring. I've made them in an infinite variety of ways, for an infinite number of occasions, and for every stage of life—from high chair to rocking chair.

Bridge club at your house tonight? Serve low-calorie Peachy Pecan Muffins. Fantastic—and not a drop of fat or concentrated sweetener. Kids passing up the vegetables? Make Carrot Orange Pecan Muffins or Zucchini Raisin and Nut Muffins, or Orange Parsnip Snowballs. Vegetables never tasted so good!

Smart Muffins are full of tasty surprises—seeds, fruits, honey, raisins, whole grains, vegetables, spices, and a number of other delectable ingredients. These nutritious loaves can be a source of pure joy—not to mention a lifesaver! An assortment of Smart Muffins tucked away in the freezer is better than money in the bank. Let the neighbors drop in. Let the kids bring their hungry friends home. Let

36

the swimmers, the joggers, the marathoners and triathloners barge in ready to eat anything that doesn't move. You'll be ready!

Smart Muffins are, of course, all natural. But according to one of my grandchildren, they have powers that supersede the natural.

Explaining to a friend one day what happens when you depart this world, she said, "God takes you up to Heaven, feeds you my grandma's muffins to make you healthy, then sends you back home."

Muffins are a joy to eat and, because they're so quick and easy, a joy to make! Here are some guidelines.

Muffin batter can be mixed by hand, mixing machine, or in a food processor. If you make them by hand, combine all the dry ingredients in one bowl, the wet ingredients in another. Make a well in the middle of the dry ingredients. Add the wet ingredients and, with a few broad strokes of a wide spatula, mix together only until the ingredients are well combined. The batter should be a little lumpy and should drop from the spoon cleanly in blobs.

Beware of overmixing. Besides causing humps, cracks, and tunnels, overmixing develops the gluten in the flour, which is fine for yeast-risen breads but not for muffins. Gluten makes for a tough-textured muffin. Mix with as few strokes as possible only until all the flour is moistened and no dry white areas of flour are visible. Add raisins, chopped dates, seeds, or nuts to the batter during the last few strokes to avoid damaging them in the mixing process.

Undermixing, on the other hand, makes for a flat-top muffin of low volume, with lumps of dry flour and a crumbly texture.

A muffin that has been mixed just enough will have a rounded top, straight sides, and an even-textured crumb, and no tunnels.

Using a Food Processor

If you are using a food processor, combine the wet ingredients in the processor bowl, and process to combine. Then add the combined dry ingredients and mix wet and dry together with 5 or 6 pushes on the processor pulse button or until no flour is visible.

Before Baking

To rise to perfection, muffins need a hot oven—about 400 degrees. Have the oven preheated to the baking temperature and muffin pans prepared before combining the wet and dry ingredients. As soon as the two mixtures are combined, hustle the batter into the prepared muffin pans and into the oven to take full advantage of the rising power of the leavening agents. Fill the cups ⅔ full and place the muffin tins in the upper half of the oven. A soup ladle makes even distribution of the batter easy. If there isn't enough batter to fill all the cups, add water to the empty ones. This makes for even heat distribution and prevents scorching of the tins.

For oversize muffins—the ones that seem to be wearing cowboy hats—fill the muffin tins almost to the top, but grease the top of the tins to prevent sticking.

Use heavyweight muffin tins for burn-resistant, fluffy results. If heavyweight muffin tins are not available, use 2 muffin tins of the same size, set inside each other.

Muffin tins can be greased with oil or butter or a mixture of liquid lecithin and oil. To have a convenient supply of this mixture on hand, mix together in a small container ¼ cup of oil and ¼ cup of liquid lecithin. Shake it up and refrigerate. It becomes semisolid and is a very convenient blend for quickly greasing your muffin tins. If you prefer, you can use paper or foil liners and you will not need to grease or wash the tins.

Plumping Raisins and Toasting Nuts

To plump raisins or any dried fruit, put the fruit in a steamer basket over about ½ cup of water. Cover and steam for about 5 minutes. Or: Pour boiling water to cover over dried fruit in a small bowl. Let soak until plumped, about a half hour. Drain well and pat dry. Or, add about a tablespoon of water or fruit juice and place in the microwave for about one minute on high.

To toast sunflower seeds or nuts, spread in a single layer on a baking sheet and toast the seeds or nuts in a 350-degree oven for about 5 minutes for seeds, 7 to 10 minutes for nuts. Shake the pan once or twice and watch them closely (they burn easily). Nuts and seeds can also be toasted in a skillet on top of the stove, using moderate heat.

Baking, Cooling, and Storing

Most regular-size muffins are done in 20 to 25 minutes, miniatures in 12 to 15 minutes. Muffins are done when a cake tester or wooden pick inserted into the center comes out clean.

Allow muffins to cool for about 5 minutes before removing them from the muffin tins; then place them on a wire rack. Allow them to cool completely before storing in refrigerator or freezer. You'll find that paper baking cups can be removed much more easily when the muffins are cool.

You can fill the house with the wonderful aroma of muffins in the oven even on hectic mornings. Simply freeze muffin batter in foil baking cups. When frozen solid, keep them in plastic bags for easier storage. Mark each package with pertinent data—like the name of the muffin, the type of flour it's made from (for the benefit of those who have allergies to certain types), whether or not it contains dairy products, and the baking temperature. Allow 10 minutes' extra time for baking.

You can also store muffin batter in the refrigerator and bake only what you need for each day's enjoyment. The batter will keep for about five days. Keep in mind, though, that the longer the batter is kept, the lower the volume of the baked muffin.

There are times when you will want to reheat muffins that have already been baked. There are several ways to keep muffins from drying out when reheating. You can cut them in halves, sprinkle each half with a few drops of water or fruit juice, then warm in a toaster oven. Or you can warm them in a steamer. You can also store baked muffins in the freezer, each one wrapped individually in foil. When reheating, place them in the oven in their foil wrappers. If, through oversight, muffins become overly dry, all is not lost. Crumble them up and use the crumbs as the base of a delicious trifle. Top the crumbs with yogurt, fruit, and nuts.

Smart Muffins Are Different

Smart Muffins are not as sweet as those your family may be accustomed to eating. Until their taste buds are educated to detect the sweetness in natural foods, serve the muffins with a conserve that adds sweetness without added sweeteners. You can make these yourself by cooking fruit in fruit juice to the consistency of apple butter, or you can buy conserves ready-made in many varieties. I like the Sorrell Ridge brand, but there are others. Read the labels. You'll find them in gourmet shops, health-food stores, and many supermarkets.

HEARTY BREAKFAST MUFFINS

Did you know . . .

- that what you eat for breakfast can affect your energy level at three in the afternoon?
- that according to a recent survey, eating a good breakfast can improve your chances of living longer?
- that eating a good breakfast means less fatigue and less fluid retention?
- that if you are skipping breakfast to lose weight, you are defeating your own purpose? Skipping breakfast keeps your metabolism in low gear. To burn fat and calories, you want to shift into high gear.

Jeffrey S. Bland, Ph.D., director of research projects for the Linus Pauling Institute of Science and author of several books, including *Your Health Under Siege: Using Nutrition to Fight Back* (Stephen Greene Press, 1981), says the ideal breakfast should be rich in complex carbohydrates and protein and contain a little fat.

Hearty Breakfast Muffins fulfill those requirements in a most delicious way. Not only do they provide complex carbohydrates for high-level energy, they also have lots of fiber for protection against polyps and cancer of the colon; seeds and nuts for important minerals, and polyunsaturated fats that keep your skin soft and lovely; whole grains with B vitamins that can actually lighten your mood, help fight stress, and sustain your energy; and spices that enhance flavors and fill the house with enticing aromas.

If you are too rushed to eat a good breakfast, slip some of these muffins into your briefcase and into the children's schoolbags. You'll find they have excellent satiety value. You won't be distracted by hunger pangs long before lunch.

Wheat Germ Raisin Ginger Muffins

Your body never had it so good! Oat bran tends to lower cholesterol. Wheat bran provides fiber, so essential to the health of your colon. Wheat germ provides vitamins that can actually improve your disposition. (It contains vitamin B_1, known as the "morale vitamin" because it helps you achieve an upbeat attitude.) It also provides pantothenic acid—known as the "antistress vitamin"—which helps you to cope with the exigencies of the morning rush hour. The spices provide a festival for your taste buds.

½ cup wheat bran	¼ cup oat bran
1 cup buttermilk or yogurt	1 teaspoon baking powder
2 large eggs	1 teaspoon baking soda
2 tablespoons olive oil	½ teaspoon ground ginger
3 tablespoons molasses or honey	½ teaspoon cinnamon
	⅛ teaspoon ground cloves
½ cup apple sauce	1 teaspoon grated orange rind
1 cup sifted whole wheat pastry flour	½ cup plumped raisins
	½ cup toasted sunflower seeds
¼ cup wheat germ	

In a small bowl, combine the bran and buttermilk or yogurt, and mix well. Set aside.

In another bowl or food processor, combine the eggs, olive oil, molasses or honey, and the applesauce. Process to combine, then add the bran mixture and process again.

Combine the flour, wheat germ, oat bran, baking powder, baking soda, and spices, and add this mixture to the wet ingredients. Process briefly just until no flour is visible. Stir in the plumped raisins.

Preheat oven to 375°F. Spoon the batter into 12 muffin cups greased with a lecithin and oil mixture. Garnish with sunflower seeds and bake for 15 to 20 minutes.

Yield: 12 muffins.

Approximately 147 calories each.

Dynamite Muffins

These high-fiber fruit-and-nut gems pack a terrific nutritional wallop and provide all the essential amino acids. They're great for breakfast on the run, backpacking, lunch boxes, or as an afternoon pickup.

1 cup orange, pineapple, or apple juice
½ cup bran
3 eggs
3 tablespoons olive oil, vegetable oil, or softened sweet butter
¼ cup molasses
1 cup applesauce
½ cup raisins, plumped
¼ cup apricots, diced
¼ cup prunes, diced
¼ cup soy flour
1½ cups whole wheat flour

½ cup dry milk powder
⅓ cup wheat germ
2 tablespoons lecithin granules
2 tablespoons oat bran
2 teaspoons baking powder
½ teaspoon baking soda
1 teaspoon cinnamon
¼ teaspoon ginger
¼ teaspoon nutmeg
1 tablespoon grated orange rind
½ cup walnuts, chopped
¼ cup peanuts, chopped

In a small bowl, combine the fruit juice and bran. Set aside.

In a large mixing bowl or food processor, mix together the eggs, oil or butter, molasses, and applesauce. Stir in the bran mixture. Add the raisins and chopped fruit.

In another bowl, stir together the flours, milk powder, wheat germ, lecithin granules, oat bran, baking powder, baking soda, spices, and orange rind.

Add the flour mixture to the wet ingredients and mix just enough to moisten the flour. Stir in the nuts.

Preheat oven to 375°F.

Grease 24 regular-size muffin cups or 5 dozen minicups with butter or a mixture of liquid lecithin and oil, or line with paper baking cups. Spoon the batter into the muffin cups. Top each with ½ pecan or ½ walnut or ¼ teaspoon blueberry or strawberry conserve.

Bake 12 minutes in the upper half of the oven for minimuffins, 20 minutes for regular-size muffins, or until lightly browned and dry inside when pierced with a cake tester or wooden pick.

Yield: 2 dozen regular-size muffins or 5 dozen minimuffins.

Approximately 124 calories each for regular-size muffins, approximately 50 calories each for minimuffins.

Wheat Sprout Muffins

You won't believe how wonderfully good-tasting these muffins are, while being loaded with life-enhancing nutrients. Wheat sprouts have an anticancer effect, according to researchers at the University of Texas. (See *Nutrition & Cancer*, Fall 1978.) Sprouting causes an explosion of nutrients, especially the vitamin B's, and increases the development of vitamin C. Teenagers love 'em.

3 eggs, separated
1 tablespoon olive or canola oil
1 tablespoon molasses
1 cup wheat sprouts

1 cup sunflower seeds
½ cup shredded coconut
1 tablespoon grated orange rind
½ cup raisins, plumped

In a mixing bowl or food processor, blend together the egg yolks, oil, and molasses. Stir in the sprouts, seeds, coconut, orange rind, and raisins. Fold in the beaten egg whites.

Preheat oven to 400°F. Line 12 regular-size muffin wells with foil baking cups, or grease with a mixture of lecithin and oil.

Spoon the batter into the muffin wells and bake for about 15 to 20 minutes or until nicely browned.

Yield: 12 muffins.

Approximately 150 calories each.

HOW TO GROW WHEAT SPROUTS

Put 4 tablespoons of wheat grains (available at health-food stores and large supermarkets) in a pint jar. Give them a quick rinse to remove surface dirt, then fill the jar ⅔ full with tepid water. Cover and let stand overnight. The next morning, cover the jar with two layers of cheesecloth secured with a rubber band, or with a screened lid available at gourmet and health-food stores. You can make your own from window screen cut to fit a jar ring.

Without removing the screened lid, pour off the soak water, but do not discard it. Use it in soup or in cooking water for vegetables, or to replace the fat in a stir-fry.

Next, rinse the grains with tepid water, pour off the rinse water (give it to your plants), and let the jar rest under the sink or on the sink, slightly tilted so excess moisture can drain off. Use a sponge or folded dishcloth to prop up the jar bottom. Cover the jar with a tea towel if you're keeping it on the sink—the grains germinate best in the dark.

Repeat the rinsing procedure 2 or 3 times throughout the next 2 days. By the end of the second day, your wheat sprouts should be almost as long as the grain and ready for use. Refrigerate them until you're ready to use them.

Follow the same procedure for other grains such as triticale and rye and for garbanzo beans (chick-peas).

Maple Walnut Muffins

The lovely flavor of maple syrup mingled with the crunch of walnuts, which permeates every bite of these muffins, always evokes for me the memory of the corner ice-cream store where maple walnut was my standard order.

2 eggs
3 tablespoons walnut oil or
   unsalted butter, softened
¼ cup maple syrup
½ cup milk
½ cup whole wheat pastry flour

¼ cup wheat germ
¼ cup oat bran
2 teaspoons baking powder
1 teaspoon baking soda
½ cup chopped walnuts

In a bowl or food processor, mix together the eggs, oil or butter, maple syrup, and milk.

In another bowl combine the pastry flour, wheat germ, bran, baking powder, and baking soda. Process briefly, then stir in the nuts.

Preheat oven to 350°F and spoon the batter into 12 muffin cups greased with a lecithin and oil mixture. Bake for 20 to 25 minutes or until toasty brown.

Yield: 12 muffins.

Approximately 127 calories each.

Date and Nut Muffins

There are lots of hardworking nutrients in these fabulous-tasting muffins. The dates contribute a lovely natural sweetness, lots of potassium (so necessary for the smooth functioning of the muscles that control the beat of your heart), and goodly amounts of calcium, iron, phosphorus, niacin, and vitamin A.

1 teaspoon baking soda
1 cup boiling water
½ cup dates, cut in thirds
½ cup raisins
2 eggs
1 teaspoon vanilla
1 tablespoon walnut, olive, or
    vegetable oil
1 tablespoon honey
1 tablespoon molasses

2 tablespoons wheat bran
1¾ cups sifted whole wheat
    pastry flour
3 tablespoons wheat germ
4 tablespoons lecithin granules
2 tablespoons oat bran
1 teaspoon baking powder
1 tablespoon grated orange
    rind
½ cup chopped walnuts

Add the baking soda to the boiling water. Soak the dates and raisins in the water for about 10 minutes or until slightly softened.

In a small bowl or food processor, blend together the eggs, vanilla, oil, honey, and molasses. Add the wheat bran and the date-raisin mixture with the liquid they were soaked in.

In another bowl, mix together the flour, wheat germ, lecithin granules, oat brans, baking powder, and orange rind.

Preheat oven to 400°F. Line 12 regular-size muffin wells with paper or foil liners, or grease with a mixture of lecithin and oil.

Combine the wet and dry ingredients and mix briefly just to moisten the dry ingredients, then stir in the nuts. Spoon into the muffin wells and bake for about 20 minutes or until a cake tester comes out clean.

Yield: 12 large muffins.

Approximately 170 calories each.

Hearty Pear and Pecan Muffins

I haven't the vaguest idea what makes these high-risers peak so perfectly. Our kids call them skyscrapers and light up like the Fourth of July when I have a batch ready for after-school snacking.

- 2 large eggs
- ¼ cup maple syrup
- 2 tablespoons olive, walnut, or vegetable oil
- ½ cup buttermilk or yogurt
- 1 teaspoon vanilla
- 2 tablespoons wheat bran
- 1½ cups sifted whole wheat pastry flour
- 2 tablespoons wheat germ
- 3 tablespoons lecithin granules
- 2 tablespoons oat bran

- 1 teaspoon baking powder
- 1 teaspoon baking soda
- 1 teaspoon cinnamon
- 1 tablespoon grated orange rind
- ⅛ teaspoon grated nutmeg
- 1½ cups coarsely chopped cored pears
- ½ cup chopped pecans (walnuts, hazelnuts, or peanuts may be substituted)

In a mixing bowl or food processor, blend together the eggs, maple syrup, oil, buttermilk or yogurt, vanilla, and wheat bran.

In another bowl, mix together the flour, wheat germ, lecithin granules, oat bran, baking powder, baking soda, cinnamon, orange rind, and nutmeg.

Preheat oven to 400°F. Line 12 regular-size muffin cups with baking liners, or grease with a mixture of lecithin and oil.

Combine the wet and dry ingredients and mix briefly, just to moisten the dry ingredients. Stir in the pears and nuts. Spoon the batter into the muffin wells and bake for about 18 minutes or until the muffins are nicely rounded, golden brown, and a cake tester comes out clean.

Yield: 12 muffins.

Approximately 161 calories each.

Fig and Nut Muffins

The fragrance of these muffins will wake up your late-for-breakfast sleepyheads. Figs have exceptional nutritional value and are easy to digest. They provide protein, fiber, vitamins A and B, and the bioflavenoids, which strengthen your cartilage. Serve plain with butter or fancy with cream cheese, cherry preserves, or orange marmalade.

½ cup chopped figs soaked in
　　¼ cup orange juice
1 cup yogurt
½ cup unprocessed bran
2 large eggs
2 tablespoons molasses
1 tablespoon honey
2 tablespoons olive oil or
　　softened butter
1½ cups sifted whole wheat
　　pastry flour

1¼ cups soy flour
2 tablespoons oat bran
1 teaspoon baking soda
1 teaspoon baking powder
1 teaspoon cinnamon
1 teaspoon grated orange rind
½ cup plumped raisins
½ cup toasted walnuts,
　　chopped
　　walnuts for garnishing

In a small bowl, combine the fig and orange juice mixture with the yogurt and bran. Set aside. In a large bowl or food processor, combine the eggs, molasses, honey, and oil or butter. Process to combine. In another bowl, combine the flours, oat bran, baking soda, baking powder, cinnamon, and orange rind.

Preheat oven to 400°F. Grease 12 muffin cups with a lecithin and oil mixture or line with paper baking cups.

Add the wet to the dry ingredients and process just long enough to combine. Stir in the raisins and nuts.

Spoon the batter into the muffin cups and garnish each muffin with ½ walnut. Bake in the upper half of the oven for about 20 minutes or until golden and a cake tester comes out clean. Allow to cool for 5 minutes, then turn out onto a rack.

Yield: 12 large muffins.

Approximately 176 calories each.

SCRUMPTIOUS BRUNCH MUFFINS

A brunch is informal, relaxing, chummy, easy on the hostess, and my favorite way to entertain, especially during the hectic holiday season, when the children are home from college, the married ones come home with a "pride" of grandchildren, and everyone wants to visit, get together with old friends and classmates, and catch up on what's new.

These brunch muffins are a little more exotic than the breakfast muffins but no less wholesome. The Peachy Beany Spice Muffins are very rich in fiber, which, by decreasing the absorption of cholesterol and unfriendly fats, significantly reduces the incidence of cardiovascular disease.

The Orange Marmalade Poppy Seed Muffins provide a good supply of zinc, which stimulates immune cell production, thus providing a measure of protection against disease.

The Wheat Sprout Muffins provide vitamin E, which helps maintain normal viscosity in the blood, thus lessening the risk of damaging blood clots.

All of these muffins freeze well, making it possible to make a variety ahead of time and be ready for any sudden invasion. Warm them in the oven to put a toasty crust on them before serving. The enticing aroma will add another dimension to the fun and cordiality.

You could make it a "muffin brunch" and serve them with an assortment of sensational toppings like yogurt cream cheese blended with strawberry conserves, banana-orange jam, or apricot-almond spread.

Peachy Beany Spice Muffins

Beans and grains have complementary amino acids that make these muffins a complete protein source. The beans contribute iron, calcium, magnesium, and fiber, and the peaches make them taste like fruitcake.

1 cup cooked pinto beans, mashed

2 tablespoons olive or vegetable oil

2 tablespoons honey or molasses

1 egg

1 teaspoon vanilla

2 tablespoons yogurt or buttermilk

½ cup sifted whole wheat pastry flour

2 tablespoons wheat germ

1 teaspoon baking powder

1 teaspoon baking soda

½ teaspoon cinnamon

¼ teaspoon nutmeg

¼ teaspoon ground cloves

1 cup diced peaches (1 large)

½ cup diced prunes

¼ cup chopped nuts

If you're using a food processor, put the beans in the processor bowl with the oil, honey or molasses, egg, and vanilla, and process until the beans are mashed.

If you're using a mixing bowl, mash the beans and blend with the oil, honey or molasses, beaten egg, vanilla, and yogurt or buttermilk.

In another bowl, combine the flour, wheat germ, baking powder, baking soda, and spices.

Preheat oven to 375°F. Stir in the fruit and nuts. Spoon the mixture into foil muffin cups and bake for about 25 minutes or until a cake tester comes out clean.

Yield: 12 muffins.

Approximately 109 calories each.

Orange Marmalade Poppy Seed Muffins

Poppy seeds are a good source of important enzymes, the B vitamins, and many minerals—including zinc, which is essential to healing, to your sense of taste, to healthy bones, and to growth in children.

1 large egg
2 tablespoons frozen orange juice concentrate (slightly thawed)
2 tablespoons honey or molasses
2 tablespoons olive oil or softened butter
½ cup yogurt or buttermilk
2 tablespoons wheat bran
⅓ cup unsweetened orange marmalade (Sorrell Ridge)
1½ cups sifted whole wheat pastry flour

3 tablespoons poppy seeds
2 tablespoons lecithin granules
2 tablespoons wheat germ
2 tablespoons oat bran
1 tablespoon grated orange rind
1 teaspoon baking powder
1 teaspoon baking soda
orange glaze (2 tablespoons orange marmalade mixed with 1 tablespoon boiling water)

In a mixing bowl or food processor, blend together the egg, orange concentrate, honey or molasses, oil or butter, yogurt or buttermilk, bran, and marmalade.

In another bowl, mix together the flour, seeds, lecithin granules, wheat germ, oat bran, orange rind, baking powder, and baking soda.

Preheat oven to 400°F. Line 12 muffin wells with paper baking cups, or grease with a mixture of lecithin and oil.

Combine the wet and dry mixtures and stir only until the dry ingredients are moistened. Spoon the batter into the muffin wells and bake for about 20 minutes or until a cake tester comes out clean. Brush the tops of the muffins with the orange glaze.

Yield: 12 muffins.

Approximately 102 calories each.

Coffee Cake Muffins

Light, fluffy, tender, crusty—fantastic! Enjoy them hot from the oven . . . and in good conscience. The lecithin and oat bran tend to lower both triglycerides and cholesterol.

BATTER

1 cup yogurt or sour cream or half of each
1 teaspoon baking soda
¼ cup sweet butter, softened
4 tablespoons honey
2 eggs
1 teaspoon vanilla

2 cups sifted whole wheat pastry flour
2 tablespoons lecithin granules
2 tablespoons wheat germ
2 tablespoons oat bran
2 teaspoons baking powder

TOPPING

½ cup unsweetened ground coconut
½ cup chopped nuts

1 teaspoon cinnamon
1 teaspoon grated orange rind

Stir the baking soda into the sour cream or yogurt and set aside.

In a mixing bowl or a food processor, blend together the butter, honey, eggs, and vanilla. Stir in the sour cream mixture.

In another bowl, mix together the pastry flour, lecithin granules, wheat germ, oat bran, and baking powder.

Preheat oven to 350°F. Grease 12 regular-size muffin cups with a lecithin and oil mixture or with butter.

Combine the topping ingredients. Put 2 tablespoons of batter in each muffin cup. Divide the topping mixture in half. Distribute half over the batter. Add the rest of the muffin batter, then top each with the rest of the topping mixture. Bake for 20 to 25 minutes.

Yield: 12 muffins.

Approximately 200 calories each.

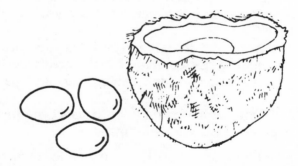

EAT-YOUR-VEGETABLES MUFFINS

Put on your thinking cap and get ready for a little trivia. What class of foods meets all the criteria for the ideal food plan—high complex carbohydrates, high fiber, high mineral and vitamin content, low fat, and low in calories?

The answer, of course, is *vegetables*.

And now, with the exciting recent studies showing the value of beta carotene as a substance that helps retard and even prevent the development of cancerous growths, the push is on to get more vegetables into our diet.

But what about taste? Many of us still harbor memories of tired, tasteless blobs of vegetables that we were coaxed to eat because there were starving children in India. And mothers across the country are still nudging and threatening, "Eat your carrots or you don't get dessert!"

The answer is to make vegetables so appealing that children will prefer them to dessert. How? Make great vegetable muffins! Carrots, sweet potatoes, zucchini, cauliflower, and peppers never tasted so good.

Here are some tips on how to select the freshest and most flavorful vegetables for your muffins:

Carrots: Look for carrots that are well formed, smooth, bright orange, and firm. Avoid roots with large green "sunburned" areas at the top. These must be cut away. And watch out for roots that are flabby or that show spots of decay.

Peppers: Look for a glossy sheen, firm walls, and a relatively heavy weight. Avoid peppers with very thin walls (they will be lighter and have flimsy sides) and those that are wilted or flabby with cuts or punctures through the walls.

Sweet potatoes: Look for well-shaped, firm sweet potatoes with smooth, bright, uniformly colored skins free from signs of decay. Avoid those with worm holes, cuts, or any other defects that penetrate the skin; these cause decay. Even if you cut away the decayed portion, the remainder of the sweet potato, though it looks normal, may have a bad taste. Store sweet potatoes in a cool, dark, dry place but not in the refrigerator.

Zucchini and other members of the squash family: Look for ones that are well developed, firm and brightly colored, with no brown patches. The skin should be glossy and not hard or tough. Avoid overmature squash with a dull appearance and a hard, tough surface.

Don't buy vegetables from the bargain basket. It's penny-foolish. A few cents extra for vegetables in top condition is a good investment.

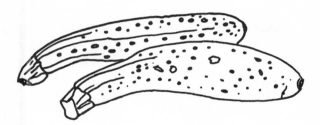

Carrot Orange Pecan Muffins

Orange concentrate and plumped raisins combine with grated carrots to bring sweetness and many palate-pleasing textures and flavors to these nutritious muffins. Carrots are loaded with vitamin A (15,600 I.U. in a cup), needed for growth and repair of body tissue. It also helps fight infection and promotes a smooth, blemish-free complexion.

2 eggs
½ cup frozen orange juice concentrate
3 tablespoons olive oil, vegetable oil, or softened butter
¼ cup buttermilk or yogurt
1½ cups grated carrot (½ pound)
½ cup chopped pecans
½ cup plumped raisins
1¼ cups sifted whole wheat flour

¼ cup wheat germ
2 tablespoons lecithin granules
2 tablespoons oat bran
1 teaspoon cinnamon
1 tablespoon grated orange rind
½ teaspoon ginger
1 teaspoon baking soda
1 teaspoon baking powder
shredded coconut for garnish

In a large bowl or food processor, blend together the eggs, orange juice concentrate, oil or butter, buttermilk or yogurt, and grated carrots. Mix in the raisins and nuts.

In another bowl, stir together the flour, wheat germ, lecithin granules, oat bran, cinnamon, orange rind, ginger, baking soda, and baking powder.

Preheat oven to 375°F. Grease or line with paper or foil cups 3 dozen minimuffin cups or 1 dozen regular-size tins.

Add the dry ingredients to the wet mixture and blend together briefly, only enough to combine. Spoon the mixture into the prepared cups; top with coconut and bake for 15 minutes.
Yield: 3 dozen minimuffins or 1 dozen regular-size muffins.
Approximately 47 calories each for minimuffins, approximately 141 calories each for regular-size muffins.

Zucchini Raisin and Nut Muffins

Don't despair if the children make a meal of these high-protein, very nutritious, deliciously moist muffins. Zucchini is rich in vitamin A and potassium and incredibly low in calories. So enjoy them in good conscience.

½ cup raisins
2 cups grated unpeeled
    zucchini
2 eggs
3 tablespoons olive or vegetable oil, or softened
    butter
¼ cup honey
1 teaspoon vanilla
1½ cups sifted whole wheat
    pastry flour

¼ cup soy flour
¼ cup oatmeal
2 tablespoons wheat germ
2 tablespoons oat bran
2 tablespoons wheat bran
2 teaspoons baking powder
1 teaspoon baking soda
1 teaspoon cinnamon
2 teaspoons grated orange rind
½ cup chopped walnuts or
    pecans

Combine the raisins and grated zucchini. Set aside.

In a mixing bowl or food processor, blend together the eggs, oil or butter, honey, and vanilla. Add the zucchini-raisin mixture.

In another bowl, mix together the flours, oatmeal, wheat germ, oat bran, wheat bran, baking powder, baking soda, cinnamon, and orange rind.

Preheat oven to 400°F. Grease 12 regular-size muffin cups with a lecithin and oil mixture or line with baking cups.

Add the dry ingredients to the wet mixture and blend together only until all the flour is moistened. Stir in the nuts. Fill the muffin cups with batter and bake for about 20 minutes.

Yield: 12 large muffins.

Approximately 189 calories each.

Potato Muffins

These savory, crisp-crusted muffins are a perfect accompaniment for a wonderful chicken dinner. Potatoes are an excellent source of energy, high in fiber, and believe it or not, low in calories—only 90 calories in a 5-ounce potato, which also provides 20 milligrams of vitamin C.

3 eggs
1 medium-size onion, diced
2 large unpeeled potatoes,
*   scrubbed and diced*
¼ cup whole wheat flour
2 tablespoons wheat germ
2 tablespoons wheat bran
2 tablespoons oat bran
2 tablespoons lecithin granules

½ teaspoon baking powder
¼ teaspoon cinnamon
⅛ teaspoon curry
½ teaspoon freshly ground
*   pepper*
2 tablespoons fresh dill
*   snipped or 1 teaspoon*
*   dried*
sesame seeds for garnish

In a blender or food processor, process the eggs, onion, and potatoes to a coarse consistency.

In a bowl, combine the wheat flour, wheat germ, wheat and oat bran, lecithin granules, baking powder, cinnamon, curry, and pepper.

Preheat oven to 400°F. Line 12 regular-size muffin tins with foil cups.

Add the dry ingredients to the potato mixture and process to blend all the ingredients. Stir in the dill.

Spoon the batter into the muffin cups and top with a sprinkle of sesame seeds. Bake for 25 to 30 minutes or until the muffins are toasty brown.

Yield: 12 muffins.

Approximately 65 calories each.

Orange Parsnip Snowballs

Sweet parsnips accented with tangy orange juice, golden raisins, crunchy coconut, and pecans or walnuts make these muffins deliciousy wholesome. Parsnips provide more potassium and more calcium than bananas. Coconut provides potassium, iron, and traces of the B vitamins.

1 cup grated parsnip (1 large or 2 small)
⅓ cup frozen orange juice concentrate
½ cup orange juice
2 eggs
3 tablespoons olive or vegetable oil
3 tablespoons honey
½ cup golden raisins, plumped
1½ cups sifted whole wheat pastry flour

½ cup rolled oats
3 tablespoons wheat germ
1 teaspoon baking soda
1 teaspoon baking powder
1 teaspoon cinnamon
1 tablespoon grated orange rind
½ cup chopped pecans or walnuts
flaked, unsweetened coconut for garnish

In a mixing bowl or food processor, blend together the grated parsnip, orange juice concentrate and juice, eggs, oil, and honey. Stir in the raisins.

In another bowl, mix together the flour, oats, wheat germ, baking soda, baking powder, cinnamon, and orange rind.

Preheat oven to 400°F. Grease 12 regular-size muffin cups with a lecithin and oil mixture. Sprinkle coconut in each muffin cup.

Add the dry ingredients to the parsnip mixture and blend only until no flour is visible. Stir in the nuts.

NOTE: To grate the parsnip, scrub it well but do not peel. Use a hand grater or food processor, using a steel blade.

Spoon the batter into the muffin cups. Top each muffin with a sprinkle of coconut. Bake for 18 to 20 minutes.

Yield: 12 muffins.

Approximately 191 calories each.

Remarkable Yellow Pepper Muffins

Yellow peppers are incredibly sweet and nutrient-dense, providing more vitamin C than most oranges, lots of carotene, potassium, vitamin A, some calcium, iron, and the vitamin B's. And they're ridiculously low in calories. Flax seed is a rich source of omega 3 fatty acids, the kind that are good for your heart and arteries.

1 cup diced yellow pepper
1 egg
1 tablespoon olive or vegetable
   oil
2 tablespoons honey
1 tablespoon molasses
½ cup buttermilk or yogurt
1 cup whole wheat pastry
   flour
2 tablespoons wheat bran

3 tablespoons wheat germ
2 tablespoons oat bran
1 tablespoon flax seed
1 tablespoon grated orange
   rind
1 teaspoon cinnamon
⅛ teaspoon nutmeg
   pinch of ginger
½ cup currants
¼ cup chopped walnuts

Purée the pepper in a food processor, using a metal blade.

Add to the puréed pepper the egg, oil, honey, molasses, and buttermilk or yogurt, and process to blend all the ingredients.

In another bowl, combine the pastry flour, wheat bran, wheat germ, oat bran, flax seed, orange rind, cinnamon, nutmeg, and ginger.

Preheat oven to 400°F. Line 12 regular-size muffin wells with foil or paper baking cups, or grease with a mixture of oil and lecithin.

Combine the wet and dry mixtures and mix briefly just to blend

the ingredients. Stir in the currants and walnuts. Spoon the batter into the muffin wells and bake for 18 to 20 minutes.
Yield: 12 muffins.
Approximately 105 calories each.

Sweet Potato Maple Walnut Muffins

What a delightful way to get your beta carotene and your potassium in every delicious bite, plus a good helping of precious linoleic acid, which helps prevent harmful deposits of cholesterol and contributes to smooth, beautiful skin.

2 eggs
1/3 cup maple syrup
2 tablespoons sweet butter or
    olive oil
1/2 cup crushed, unsweetened
    pineapple with juice
1 teaspoon vanilla
1 cup grated raw sweet potato

1/2 cup raisins, plumped
1/2 cup sunflower seeds or
    chopped walnuts
1 3/4 cups sifted whole wheat flour
1/4 cup wheat germ
2 teaspoons baking powder
1 teaspoon cinnamon
1/8 teaspoon ground nutmeg

In a large bowl or food processor, blend together the eggs, maple syrup, butter or olive oil, pineapple, vanilla, sweet potato, raisins, and walnuts or sunflower seeds.

In another bowl, stir together the wheat flour, wheat germ, baking powder, cinnamon, and nutmeg.

Preheat oven to 375°F. Grease or line 3 dozen minimuffin wells or 1 dozen regular-size muffin wells.

Combine the wet and dry ingredients and mix only enough to combine the ingredients. Spoon the mixture into the prepared muffin tins. Sprinkle a few nuts or seeds on each muffin.

Bake 12 to 15 minutes for minimuffins, 20 to 25 minutes for regular-size muffins or until golden brown and a cake tester comes out clean.

Yield: 3 dozen minimuffins or 1 dozen regular-size muffins.

Approximately 50 calories each for minimuffins, approximately 179 calories each for regular-size muffins.

Herbed Corn Muffins

Irresistibly good with fish or fowl. Serve them hot and crunchy. They freeze well, so you can make them way ahead of the holiday rush. The oat bran contributes high-density lipoprotein that protects the arteries from arteriosclerosis.

2 eggs
1 cup buttermilk
1 tablespoon honey
¼ cup melted butter
1 well-packed tablespoon
    minced fresh sage or 1
    teaspoon dried
3 tablespoons minced fresh
    dill or 3 teaspoons dried

1 cup cornmeal
1 cup whole wheat pastry flour
2 tablespoons oat bran
2 tablespoons lecithin granules
    sesame or poppy seeds for
    garnish
1 teaspoon baking powder
1 teaspoon baking soda

In a mixing bowl or food processor, blend together the eggs, buttermilk, honey, and butter. Add the minced herbs.

In another bowl, mix together the cornmeal, pastry flour, oat bran, baking powder, baking soda, and lecithin granules.

Preheat oven to 400°F. Butter 12 regular-size muffin cups.

Combine the dry and wet ingredients and blend together only until no flour is visible. Fill each muffin cup ¾ full. Top with poppy or sesame seeds—or both. Bake for 12 minutes and enjoy the savory fragrance.

Yield: 12 muffins.

Approximately 144 calories each.

MEALS-IN-A-MUFFIN

You'll love having a supply of these savory muffins in the freezer. On days when you'd rather go to the gym, to the pool, or shopping, than cook a complete dinner, you'll be thankful to have these splendid, ready-to-eat meals right at your fingertips.

I consider these muffins great stress-breakers. One of the biggest stresses we face is figuring out what to have for dinner, what to bring to the covered dish supper, what to prepare for a condolence call, and what to make for the new family on the block. With these Meals-in-a-Muffin, you'll be armed for any occasion.

Meals-in-a-Muffin also provide you with an easy and delicious way to recycle your leftovers. Using these recipes as your guide, you can turn leftover potatoes, broccoli, and even holiday turkey into scrumptious muffins to enjoy now or later.

The Tuna Melt Muffins and the Pizza Muffins are favorites with my grandchildren. When they barge in, cold and hungry after a long trip, I pop a tray of these muffins into the oven and have them ready by the time the kids have hugged everybody and hung up their coats.

Zesty Black Bean and Rice Muffins

Marvelous for a cocktail party or as an appetizer to heighten your dining experience. The combination of black beans and rice was introduced to us by Carla, our Brazilian daughter, who spent a year with us as an exchange student. She liked to put slices of banana on top for a contrast in flavor. Beans and rice have complementary amino acids, making the combination a complete protein.

*1 cup cooked black turtle
    beans
1 cup brown rice
¼ cup chopped fresh parsley
½ teaspoon curry powder
1 clove garlic, crushed*

*1 tablespoon tamari soy sauce
1 small egg
2 tablespoons sunflower seeds
    ground to a flour
½ to ¾ cup sesame seeds*

In a mixing bowl, combine all the ingredients except the sesame seeds. Mix well with a fork.

Preheat oven to 350°F and line a 2-dozen minimuffin tin with paper or foil liners.

Form the mixture into walnut-size balls and roll in the sesame seeds. Place the balls in the muffin cups and bake for 10 to 15 minutes. These can be served hot or cold.

Yield: 2 dozen minimuffins.

Approximately 46 calories each.

Blintz Muffins

Served fresh from the oven or at room temperature, these high-protein muffins and a salad make a satisfying meal. They also make a substantial lunch box treat. Eggs are an excellent source of protein, vitamins A, B, E, and K, and are one of the few foods that provide vitamin D, so essential to the utilization of calcium.

3 eggs
1 cup cottage cheese
3 tablespoons sour cream
2 tablespoons honey
1 teaspoon vanilla
½ cup whole wheat pastry
   flour

2 tablespoons wheat germ
2 tablespoons lecithin granules
1 tablespoon grated orange
   rind
½ teaspoon cinnamon
   sliced almonds for garnish

In a mixing bowl or food processor, blend together the eggs, cheese, sour cream, honey, and vanilla.

In another bowl, combine the pastry flour, wheat germ, lecithin granules, orange rind, and cinnamon.

Preheat oven to 350°F. Grease 12 regular-size muffin cups, or 3 dozen minicups, or line with foil baking cups.

Spoon the batter into the cups. Top each muffin with a few slices of almonds. Bake regular-size muffins for 25 minutes, minimuffins for 15 to 18 minutes.

Yield: 12 regular-size muffins or 36 minimuffins.

Approximately 73 calories each for regular-size muffins, approximately 24 calories each for minimuffins.

Pizza Muffins

You simply must try these muffins. They rise up high and look gorgeous in their tomato and cheese top hats. The kids go gaga for them. To serve, split them in halves and serve hot and topped with mozzarella cheese.

1 egg
½ cup tomato sauce
1 cup buttermilk or yogurt
4 slices mozzarella cheese, cut in dice
¼ teaspoon freshly ground pepper
1 teaspoon crushed dry oregano leaf

¼ teaspoon garlic powder
1½ cups whole wheat pastry flour
3 tablespoons wheat germ
2 teaspoons baking powder
1 teaspoon baking soda
sliced tomatoes and more cheese for garnish
sesame seeds

In a mixing bowl or food processor, blend together the egg, tomato sauce, and buttermilk or yogurt. Add the cheese and the spices. In another bowl, mix together the pastry flour, wheat germ, baking powder, and baking soda.

Preheat oven to 400°F. Butter or grease with a lecithin and oil mixture 12 regular-size muffin cups.

Combine the two mixtures and mix until no flour is visible. Spoon the batter into the muffin cups and top each muffin with a slice of tomato, cover it with cheese, and sprinkle sesame seeds on top. Bake for 20 to 25 minutes.

Yield: 12 muffins.

Approximately 88 calories each.

Mushroom Broccoli Cheese Muffins

Broccoli is the most nutrient-dense food in the marketplace, with twice as much vitamin C as orange juice and with potassium, lots of calcium and vitamin A, and some B vitamins. All this goodness at a cost of only 26 calories in 3½ ounces. Even vegetable-scorners flip for these nutrient-rich, low-calorie treats.

2 cups lightly steamed
    chopped broccoli
½ cup grated cheddar or
    mozzarella cheese
½ cup chopped onions
1 cup chopped mushrooms
2 tablespoons butter
2 tablespoons whole wheat
    pastry flour
½ cup water

2 eggs
3 tablespoons wheat germ
4 tablespoons whole wheat
    flour
¼ teaspoon pepper
1 teaspoon crushed leaf
    oregano
sesame seeds and more
    cheese for garnish

Combine the broccoli and the cheese and set aside. Sauté the onions and mushrooms in the butter. Stir in the 2 tablespoons of pastry flour and add the water. Cook slowly until the sauce thickens.

In a mixing bowl or food processor, blend together the eggs, wheat germ, remaining flour, pepper, and oregano.

Preheat oven to 400°F. Butter or grease with a lecithin and oil mixture 12 regular-size muffin cups. Sprinkle sesame seeds on the bottom of each.

Combine the broccoli-cheese mixture with the other mixture. Spoon

into the muffin cups. Top each with a sprinkle of sesame seeds and cheese. Bake for 20 minutes.
Yield: 12 muffins.
Approximately 91 calories each.

Hearty Kasha Mushroom Cheese Muffins

Kasha is roasted buckwheat groats. It looks like a grain but is not. It is related to the rhubarb family, has a hearty flavor, and is an excellent source of iron. Mushrooms help you to cope. They are rich in pantothenic acid, the antistress vitamin.

1 medium onion, chopped
1 cup chopped mushrooms
1 cup chopped zucchini
  (optional)
1 tablespoon butter
1 cup cooked kasha (buck-
  wheat groats)
2 eggs, beaten
½ cup cottage cheese
¼ cup wheat germ
¼ cup whole wheat pastry
  flour

½ teaspoon baking powder
½ teaspoon curry powder
1 teaspoon dried thyme or 1
  tablespoon fresh
1 teaspoon vegetable seasoning or to taste
grated cheddar cheese, sliced
  almonds, and paprika
  for garnish

Sauté the onion, mushrooms, and zucchini in the butter. Mix in the kasha, cottage cheese, and eggs.

In another bowl, combine the wheat germ, pastry flour, baking powder, curry powder, thyme, and vegetable seasoning.

Preheat oven to 400°F. Grease 12 regular-size muffin tins with butter or a lecithin and oil mixture.

Combine the wet and dry mixtures. Stir briefly to blend. Spoon the batter into the muffin cups. Sprinkle with cheese, paprika, and almonds. Bake for 20 minutes.

Yield: 12 muffins.

Approximately 74 calories each.

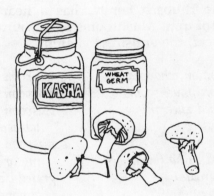

Corny Potato Sunflower Muffins

These are a must for holiday meals. The aroma as they are baking raises the cockles on appetites. They taste like knishes. Potatoes are a good source of fiber. Serve them piping hot.

2 medium-size onions, chopped
½ cup sunflower seeds
1 tablespoon butter or oil
1 cup corn niblets
2 cups mashed potatoes
2 eggs

¼ cup whole wheat pastry flour
¼ cup wheat germ
¼ teaspoon baking powder
½ teaspoon freshly grated pepper
¼ teaspoon grated nutmeg
sprinkle of paprika

Sauté the onions and sunflower seeds in the butter or oil. Add the corn.

In a bowl, combine the mashed potatoes, 1 egg, and 1 egg white. Reserve the other yolk.

Combine the pastry flour, wheat germ, and baking powder and add to the mashed potatoes. Combine this mixture with the onion mixture. Add the spices.

Preheat oven to 400°F. Grease 12 muffin cups with a lecithin and oil mixture.

Spoon the mixture into the muffin cups. Brush each muffin with egg yolk. Bake for 20 minutes or until golden brown.

Yield: 12 muffins.

Approximately 105 calories each.

Corny Corn and Chive Muffins

Serve these muffins hot with a hearty bowl of soup or chowder and you've got a meal. Corn is low in fat, high in fiber, and provides potassium, vitamin A, and niacin, which tends to lower cholesterol.

2 eggs
1 cup buttermilk or yogurt
2 tablespoons softened butter
    or olive or vegetable oil
2 tablespoons minced fresh
    chives or 2 teaspoons
    dried
1 cup corn, scraped from a
    cooked cob, or frozen
    corn, thawed, or canned
    corn, drained

1½ cups yellow cornmeal
¼ cup whole wheat flour
2 tablespoons wheat germ
2 tablespoons wheat or oat
    bran
1 tablespoon baking powder
1 teaspoon baking soda
    mozzarella or cheddar
    cheese and sesame seeds
    for garnish

In a mixing bowl or food processor, blend the eggs, buttermilk or yogurt, butter or oil, and the chives. Add the corn kernels.

In another bowl, combine the cornmeal, flour, wheat germ, bran, baking powder, and baking soda.

Preheat oven to 400°F. Grease 12 regular-size muffin cups with a lecithin and oil mixture or line with foil baking cups.

Spoon 2 tablespoons of batter into each cup. Place a piece of cheese on each, then the rest of the batter on top of the cheese. Place another small piece of cheese on top of each muffin and top with a sprinkle of sesame seeds. Bake for 20 minutes.

Yield: 12 muffins.

Approximately 123 calories each.

Matzo Meal Muffins

Eggs are the only leavening in these muffins, which are acceptable for Passover but welcome anytime. Serve hot with butter, cream cheese, or fruit conserve, or plain, dunked in chicken soup.

3 eggs, separated
1 tablespoon grated orange
rind

1 cup cold water
1½ cups matzo meal

In a mixing bowl or mixing machine, beat the egg whites until they form peaks. Continue beating as you dribble in the egg yolks.

Add the orange rind to the matzo meal. Add the matzo meal mixture and water alternately to the beaten eggs.

Preheat oven to 400°F. Line 12 regular-size muffin wells with foil baking cups or grease with oil.

Spoon the batter into the muffin wells and bake for about 30 minutes or until a cake tester comes out clean.

Yield: 12 muffins.

Approximately 76 calories each.

Variation: Use chicken broth instead of water and serve with chicken soup.

Tuna Apple Almond Muffins

Here's a versatile muffin. Terrific for lunch boxes, wholesome after-school snacks, wonderful for buffets, and a welcome bring-along dish. Oats and oat bran have been shown to lower cholesterol levels.

1 6½- or 7-ounce can tuna
    packed in water, drained
½ cup finely chopped celery
½ cup chopped apple
½ cup rolled oats (preferably
    uncooked)
2 tablespoons oat bran

½ cup chopped, roasted
    almonds or sunflower
    seeds
2 eggs, lightly beaten
⅛ teaspoon pepper
½ cup milk

DILL SAUCE

½ cup plain yogurt
½ cup chopped cucumber
2 tablespoons chopped fresh
    dill or 1 teaspoon dried

1 teaspoon minced onion

To make the sauce: In a small bowl, combine all ingredients and mix well. Chill.

To make the muffins: In a medium-size bowl, blend the tuna, then add the celery, apple, oats and oat bran, almonds or sunflower seeds, eggs, pepper, and milk.

Preheat oven to 350°F. Line 12 regular-size muffin wells with foil liners.

Spoon the batter into the muffin wells and bake for 20 to 25 minutes. Serve warm, cold, or hot from the oven with dill sauce.
Yield: 12 muffins.
Approximately 100 calories each with 2 tablespoons of sauce, approximately 98 calories each without sauce.

Turkey Cranberry Almond Muffins

I always plan to have turkey or chicken left over so I can treat my family to these crunchy, wholesome muffins. I serve them in good consience because they provide high-quality protein, plenty of the vitamin B's, and flavor that puts a smile on every face.

¼ to ½ cup turkey gravy
1 cup chopped onions
1 cup chopped celery
2 cloves garlic, minced
2 tablespoons chopped parsley
4 fresh sage leaves, chopped,
    or ¼ teaspoon dry sage
1½ cups turkey, cut in bite-size
    pieces
1 cup cooked brown rice
1 cup chopped roasted almonds

1 egg, beaten
a piece of ginger, dry
    mustard, and nutmeg
½ teaspoon curry powder
½ teaspoon dried thyme
¼ cup cranberry sauce con-
    serve (Sorrell Ridge,
    unsweetened) or your
    own cranberry sauce
1 mellow banana, mashed
    (optional)

Heat a large skillet, add the gravy, and sauté the onions and celery. Add the garlic, parsley, sage, turkey, rice, almonds, egg, spices, and cranberry sauce (banana can be added if desired).

Preheat oven to 350°F. Line regular-size muffin wells with foil baking cups. Spoon the batter into the cups, top each with a dab of cranberry sauce, and bake for 20 minutes.

Yield: 12 muffins.

Approximately 130 calories each.

Tuna Melt Muffins

Teenagers flip for these. They love to find them all ready for the toaster on days when you can't be there to greet them. Tuna provides more protein than an equal amount of porterhouse steak and is much kinder on your arteries and your budget.

1 tablespoon butter
1 tablespoon olive or vegetable oil
1 medium-size onion, minced
2 stalks celery, diced, about 1 cup
1 green or red pepper, diced
½ cup chopped almonds
¼ cup minced fresh parsley
2 cans water-packed tuna fish (6½ or 7 ounces each)
2 tablespoons lemon juice
2 eggs, beaten
½ cup sour cream or yogurt
½ cup whole wheat pastry flour
3 tablespoons wheat germ
2 tablespoons oat bran
2 tablespoons lecithin granules
1 teaspoon baking powder
¼ teaspoon freshly ground pepper
mozzarella cheese for topping

In a large skillet, heat the butter and oil. Sauté the onion briefly, then add the celery, pepper, and almonds. Add the parsley when the other ingredients are almost completely sautéed.

In another bowl, mix together the tuna, lemon juice, eggs, sour cream or yogurt, pastry flour, wheat germ, oat bran, lecithin granules, baking powder, and pepper.

Preheat oven to 375°F. Grease 12 regular-size muffin cups with a butter or lecithin and oil mixture.

Combine the tuna mixture with the sautéed ingredients. Spoon the mixture into the muffin cups. Top each muffin with a piece of cheese. Bake for 20 minutes.

Yield: 12 muffins.

Approximately 170 calories each.

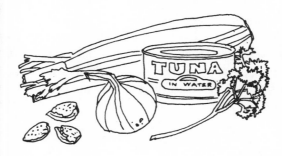

Salmon Rice Almond Muffins

Serve these muffins hot with yogurt dill sauce for a delectable main dish. Brown rice is a wonderful source of complex carbohydrates for energy and stamina. Salmon is a good source of Max EPA, the polyunsaturated fat that lowers cholesterol levels in the blood.

1 egg
¼ cup yogurt
1 small onion, chopped or grated if you're not using a processor
2 small potatoes, parboiled in their jackets, mashed if you're not using a food processor
1 7½-ounce can salmon with bones and skin or ¾ to 1 cup flaked salmon left over from dinner

1 cup cooked brown rice
2 tablespoons chopped fresh dill or 2 teaspoons dried
¼ teaspoon freshly ground pepper
grating of nutmeg
2 tablespoons whole wheat flour
2 tablespoons wheat germ
½ teaspoon baking soda
½ cup slivered almonds
sesame seeds, cheese, and paprika for garnish

In a mixing bowl or food processor, blend together the egg, yogurt, onion, potatoes, salmon, rice, dill, pepper, and nutmeg. Stir in the rice.

In another bowl, combine the flour, wheat germ, baking soda, and almonds.

Preheat oven to 375°F. Line 12 muffin cups with foil baking cups or grease with a mixture of lecithin and oil.

Combine the salmon mixture and the flour mixture. Mix only until the dry ingredients are moistened. Spoon the mixture into the muffin

cups. Top with sesame seeds and cheese, and dust with paprika. Bake for 25 to 30 minutes or until golden brown.
Yield: 12 muffins.

Approximately 120 calories each.

Variation: Use haddock, scrod, cod, or any fish you can salvage from dinner. I always buy more than I need for dinner so I have enough left over for these muffins.

Vegetarian Meal-in-a-Muffin

Tofu and brown rice team up with crisp vegetables and walnuts for a delectable oriental flavor. Two of these muffins with a salad make a satisfying, high-energy meal. Tofu (derived from soybeans) is high in protein without the fat that usually accompanies high-protein foods. Tofu also provides lecithin and choline, both of which jog the memory.

1 to 2 tablespoons olive or vegetable oil
1 cup tofu, cut in dice
1 cup chopped onion
1 cup chopped celery
1 cup chopped zucchini
2 large cloves of garlic, minced
½ cup chopped walnuts
1 cup cooked brown rice
1 egg plus one egg yolk
2 teaspoons brown rice vinegar

3 tablespoons tamari soy sauce
2 teaspoons lemon juice
¼ teaspoon ground ginger or more to taste
3 tablespoons brown rice polish or flour
2 tablespoons sesame seeds slivered almonds or whole cashews for garnish

In a large skillet or wok, heat the oil and sauté the tofu until lightly browned. Remove the tofu and sauté the onion, celery, and zucchini. (Add a little water or gravy if necessary.) Add the minced garlic, walnuts, and rice.

In another bowl, combine the egg and extra yolk, vinegar, tamari, lemon juice, and ginger.

Preheat oven to 375°F. Line 12 muffin wells with foil baking cups.

Add the rice polish or flour and sesame seeds to the tofu mixture. Fill the muffin cups and garnish each with the nuts. Bake for 18 to 20 minutes.

Yield: 12 muffins.

Approximately 120 calories each.

GO ANYWHERE FRUIT 'N' NUT MUFFINS

Right now there's snow on the ground, but I can go to my freezer for muffins made from the luscious peaches we picked last summer. Blueberries, too, that we picked in August are nestled in muffins stored in our freezer and brighten our Sunday brunches with the taste of summer's bounty. Every mouthful of these muffins is crunchy with nuts and deliciously moist with flavorful fruit. As one of my grandchildren remarked, "They make music in my mouth!"

I use fruit in muffins not only for the marvelous flavor and texture it adds but also because of its vitamin and mineral content, which has a refreshing and restorative effect. For example, fruit is an excellent source of pectin, which helps to usher toxic chemicals out of the body.

Nuts are perfect companions for fruits, providing complementary amino acids, thus enriching the protein value of the muffins. Nuts also provide B vitamins, important minerals, and the essential fatty acids that have been shown to lower cholesterol levels and strengthen the immune system.

Cherry Almond Amaretto Muffins

Make these for very special occasions—they delight the eye and the palate. If you are a teetotaler, you can still enjoy these muffins. The alcohol evaporates in the heat, leaving the lovely Amaretto flavor in every luscious morsel.

½ cup chopped pitted Bing
   cherries
¼ cup Amaretto liqueur
2 eggs
2 tablespoons olive or vegetable
   oil
3 tablespoons honey
¼ teaspoon almond extract
¾ cup apple-raspberry or other
   fruit juice
2 tablespoons Amaretto liqueur

1½ cups sifted whole wheat
   pastry flour
2 tablespoons wheat germ
2 tablespoons oat bran
2 tablespoons lecithin granules
1 teaspoon baking powder
1 teaspoon baking soda
½ cup chopped almonds
   sliced almonds and cherry
   halves for garnish

In a small bowl, combine the cherries and Amaretto. Set aside. In a mixing bowl or food processor, blend the eggs, oil, honey, almond extract, fruit juice, and two tablespoons of additional Amaretto. Stir in the cherry mixture.

In another bowl, combine the pastry flour, wheat germ, oat bran, lecithin granules, baking powder, and baking soda.

Preheat oven to 400°F. Grease 12 average-size muffin cups with a lecithin and oil mixture or line with paper or foil cups.

Add the dry ingredients to the cherry mixture and blend just enough to moisten the pastry flour mixture. Stir in the chopped

almonds. Spoon the mixture into muffin cups and top with sliced almonds and a piece of cherry. Bake for 20 minutes.
Yield: 12 muffins.
Approximately 175 calories each.

Banana Maple Walnut Muffins

Moist, tender, and full of flavor, these potassium-rich muffins are a favorite with our children. Be sure to use very ripe bananas, the kind that just won't last until tomorrow.

¼ cup wheat bran
¼ cup yogurt
2 eggs
2 tablespoons vegetable or olive oil
3 tablespoons maple syrup
1 cup mashed bananas (about 3 medium)
1 tablespoon lemon juice
½ cup plumped raisins
1 cup sifted whole wheat pastry flour

½ cup wheat germ
½ teaspoon baking powder
½ teaspoon baking soda
1 teaspoon ground cinnamon
1 teaspoon grated orange rind (optional)
½ cup chopped walnuts nuts or sunflower seeds for garnish

In a small bowl, mix together the yogurt and bran. Set aside.

In a mixing bowl or food processor, blend together the eggs, oil, maple syrup, mashed bananas, and lemon juice. Add the yogurt-bran mixture and the raisins.

In another bowl, mix together the pastry flour, wheat germ, baking powder, baking soda, cinnamon, and orange rind.

Preheat oven to 375°F. Grease 12 regular-size muffin cups or 36 minimuffin cups with a lecithin and oil mixture or line with foil baking cups.

Add the dry ingredients to the banana mixture and process briefly—only until no pastry flour is visible. Stir in the nuts.

Spoon the batter into the prepared muffin cups. Top each with a piece of nut or a few sunflower seeds. Bake for 20 minutes or until tinged with a golden glow.

Yield: 12 regular-size muffins or 36 minimuffins.

Approximately 150 calories each for regular-size muffins, approximately 50 calories each for minimuffins.

Apricot Almond Muffins

A marvelous muffin—good-looking, good-tasting, and richly endowed with so many important nutrients. Almonds contribute protein, potassium, iron, calcium, and polyunsaturated fatty acids. They are an excellent complement to raisins and apricots, which provide vitamin A and iron.

12 almonds	1 cup rolled oats
12 dried apricots	2 tablespoons oat bran
3 tablespoons honey	2 teaspoons baking powder
2 eggs	1 teaspoon baking soda
2 tablespoons olive or vegetable oil	½ cup dried apricots, finely chopped
⅔ cup buttermilk or yogurt	⅓ cup raisins, plumped
1 teaspoon vanilla	
1 cup sifted whole wheat pastry flour	

Soak the almonds and apricots overnight in enough water to cover them. Purée the almonds and apricots with their liquid in a food processor, then add and blend the honey, eggs, oil, buttermilk or yogurt, and vanilla.

In another bowl, mix together the pastry flour, oats, oat bran, baking powder, and baking soda.

Preheat oven to 400°F. Line 12 regular-size muffin wells with paper or foil baking cups, or grease with a mixture of lecithin and oil.

Combine the wet and dry mixtures and stir only until the dry ingredients are moistened. Fold in the apricots and raisins.

Spoon the batter into the muffin cups and bake for 15 to 20 minutes or until a cake tester comes out clean.
Yield: 12 large muffins.
Approximately 153 calories each.

Plum and Peanut Muffins

Preserve the flavor of juicy summer plums in these moist, crunchy muffins that provide lots of protein, calcium, potassium, and vitamin A.

½ cup chopped plums
½ cup apple or apple-apricot juice
2 eggs
2 tablespoons olive or vegetable oil
2 tablespoons honey
2 tablespoons molasses
1 cup sifted whole wheat flour

2 tablespoons wheat germ
2 tablespoons wheat bran
2 tablespoons oat bran
2 tablespoons soy granules or TVP (textured vegetable protein)
1 teaspoon baking powder
1 teaspoon baking soda
½ cup chopped peanuts

Add the plums to the juice to soak for about 15 minutes. In a mixing bowl or food processor, blend the eggs, oil, honey, molasses, and plums together with the juice in which they were soaked.

In another bowl, blend together the flour, wheat germ, wheat bran, oat bran, soy granules or TVP, baking powder, and baking soda.

Preheat oven to 400°F. Line 12 regular-size muffin wells with foil or paper liners, or grease with a mixture of lecithin and oil.

Combine the wet and dry mixtures and blend briefly, only until the ingredients are well combined. Stir in the peanuts. Spoon the batter into the muffin wells and bake for about 20 minutes or until a cake tester comes out clean.

Yield: 12 muffins.

Approximately 110 calories each.

Papaya Pumpkin Seed Muffins

Pumpkin seeds are rich in zinc, a mineral essential to growth, to healing, to strong bones, and to the male prostate gland. Pumpkin seeds also contribute protein and crunch to these sweet papaya muffins.

½ cup dried papaya, diced
¾ cup apple or apple-apricot
    juice
2 medium-size eggs
2 tablespoons olive or walnut
    oil
2 tablespoons molasses
1 tablespoon honey
2 tablespoons wheat bran
1 cup sifted whole wheat
    pastry flour

2 tablespoons wheat germ
½ teaspoon baking soda
1 teaspoon baking powder
1 teaspoon cinnamon
⅛ teaspoon nutmeg
    pinch of ginger
⅓ cup toasted pumpkin seeds
    pumpkin seeds for garnish

Soak the papaya in the apple juice for an hour, or overnight.

In a mixing bowl or food processor, blend together the eggs, oil, molasses, honey, wheat bran, and the juice in which the papaya was soaked.

In another bowl, mix together the pastry flour, wheat germ, baking soda, baking powder, and spices.

Preheat oven to 400°F. Line 12 muffin wells with paper or foil baking cups, or grease with a mixture of lecithin and oil.

Mix together the wet and dry ingredients only until the ingredients are well combined. Stir in the papaya and the pumpkin seeds. Spoon the batter into the muffin wells. Top each muffin with a few pumpkin seeds. Bake for 12 to 15 minutes or until a cake tester comes out clean.

Yield: 12 muffins.

Approximately 117 calories each.

Apple Pecan Bran Muffins

Apples contribute pectin and crunchy moistness to these hearty muffins. Bran provides lots of fiber, which protects against bowel diseases and decreases absorption of cholesterol, thus reducing the incidence of cardiovascular disease. For added sweetness, toast these muffins and serve with apple butter.

2 large eggs
2 tablespoons olive or vegetable
    oil
1 cup buttermilk or yogurt
3 tablespoons molasses
2 tablespoons honey or barley
    malt
⅓ cup wheat bran
1½ cups sifted whole wheat
    pastry flour

½ cup rolled oats
2 teaspoons baking powder
1 teaspoon baking soda
2 teaspoons cinnamon
¼ teaspoon ginger
¼ teaspoon nutmeg
1 apple, chopped
½ cup chopped pecans

In a mixing bowl or food processor, blend together the eggs, oil, buttermilk or yogurt, molasses, and honey or barley malt. Stir in the wheat bran.

In another bowl, mix together the pastry flour, oats, baking powder, baking soda, cinnamon, ginger, and nutmeg.

Preheat oven to 400°F. Grease 12 regular-size muffin wells with a lecithin and oil mixture or line with baking cups.

Combine the 2 mixtures and mix briefly just until the ingredients are well blended. Then stir in the apple and pecans.

Spoon the batter into the muffin cups and bake for 20 to 25 minutes or until a cake tester comes out clean.
Yield: 12 muffins.
Approximately 146 calories each.

Blueberry Sunflower Muffins

Blueberries and muffins go together like love and marriage. Blueberries are rich in manganese, a mineral essential to healthy ligaments, and believe it or not, to mother love! (Animals deficient in manganese refuse to nurture their young.) If you use frozen berries, add another ¼ cup flour.

2 *eggs*
¼ *cup honey*
2 *tablespoons softened*
   unsalted butter, or olive
   or vegetable oil
½ *cup buttermilk or yogurt*
1 *teaspoon vanilla*
1 *cup sifted whole wheat*
   pastry flour

2 *tablespoons wheat germ*
2 *tablespoons oat bran*
1 *teaspoon baking powder*
1 *teaspoon baking soda*
1½ *cups blueberries*
½ *cup sunflower seeds*

In a mixing bowl or food processor, combine the eggs, honey, oil or butter, buttermilk or yogurt, and vanilla. In another bowl, combine the pastry flour, wheat germ, oat bran, baking powder, and baking soda. Stir in the blueberries.

Preheat oven to 350°F. Grease 12 regular-size muffin cups with a lecithin and oil mixture, or line with foil or paper baking cups.

Combine the two mixtures. Stir in the sunflower seeds. Spoon the batter into the muffin cups and bake for 20 minutes.

Yield: 12 muffins.

Approximately 146 calories each.

Banana Muffins with Hazelnut Topping

These high-potassium, high-energy treats are great for lunch boxes, for afternoon tea, or for breakfast or brunch. Spread with a blend of cottage cheese and peach or banana.

2 eggs
2 bananas (about ¾ cup)
3 tablespoons honey or
    molasses
2 tablespoons olive or vegetable
    oil
½ cup yogurt, buttermilk, or
    soured milk
1¼ cups sifted whole wheat
    pastry flour

2 tablespoons oat bran
2 tablespoons wheat germ
2 tablespoons wheat bran
½ teaspoon cinnamon
1 teaspoon baking powder
1 teaspoon baking soda
    chopped hazelnuts

In a mixing bowl or food processor, blend together the eggs, bananas, honey or molasses, oil, and yogurt, buttermilk, or soured milk.

In another bowl, mix together the pastry flour, oat bran, wheat germ, wheat bran, cinnamon, baking powder, and baking soda.

Preheat oven to 400°F. Grease the bottoms of 12 regular-size muffin pan cups with a mixture of lecithin and oil or line them with paper baking cups.

Combine the dry ingredients with the banana mixture and mix briefly, only until no flour is visible. Spoon the batter into the muffin cups. Top each muffin with chopped hazelnuts. Bake for 20 to 22 minutes or until the tops are golden. Cool for 5 minutes, then remove to a wire rack.

Yield: 12 muffins.

Approximately 120 calories each.

VERY SKINNY SMART MUFFINS

All of the muffins in this book provide fewer calories than their commercial counterparts because they are low in fat and sweeteners. In this chapter, we've trimmed the calories even further, but without reducing the nutritional value. We do this by using vitamin- and mineral-rich foods that are low in calories, such as zucchini, wheat sprouts, tofu, peaches, and popcorn flour.

Cutting calories doesn't mean sacrificing taste, texture, and the joy of eating. The Heavenly Cheesecake Muffins taste like a zillion calories but have only 22. That's less than you imbibe when you eat a quarter of an apple!

The prize you get with these Very Skinny Smart Muffins is much more gratifying—good-tasting treats and a figure fit for a bikini.

Peachy Pecan Muffins

I make these muffins when peaches are ripe and plentiful, then store some in the freezer to enjoy in the middle of winter. They're great for an evening of playing Trivial Pursuit.

1 egg
2 tablespoons vegetable or olive oil
2 tablespoons honey
1 cup peach purée (1 large ripe peach whizzed in the food processor)
½ cup yogurt
½ cup rolled oats, uncooked
1¼ cups whole wheat pastry flour
2 tablespoons wheat germ
2 tablespoons oat bran
2 tablespoons wheat bran
1 tablespoon grated orange peel
2 teaspoons baking powder
1 teaspoon baking soda
1 cup chopped peaches
peach conserve (Sorrell Ridge is a good brand—only 14 calories)
chopped pecans

In a mixing bowl or food processor, blend together the egg, oil, honey, peach purée, and yogurt.

In another bowl, mix together the oats, pastry flour, wheat germ, brans, orange peel, baking powder, and baking soda.

Preheat oven to 400°F. Line 12 regular-size muffin wells with paper baking cups or grease with a mixture of lecithin and oil.

Combine the dry ingredients and the peach mixture, stirring just until blended. Stir in the chopped peaches.

Spoon the batter into the muffin cups. Top each muffin with about ½ teaspoon of conserve if you are using it, then top each with a

sprinkle of pecans. Bake for 20 to 25 minutes or until a cake tester comes out clean.
Yield: 12 muffins.
Approximately 94 calories each, without the topping; approximately 101 calories each, with peach conserve; approximately 106 calories each, with chopped almonds and conserve.

Tofu Cashew Cheeseless Cheesecake Muffins

This is a high-protein, low-calorie nosh that tastes deliciously fattening. These muffins have a creamy consistency that improves with age. Keep refrigerated and serve cold.

¼ cup raisins
¼ cup apple or apple-apricot
    juice
2 tablespoons tahini
1 teaspoon vanilla
1 tablespoon grated orange
    rind

2 tablespoons honey
1 tablespoon lemon juice
1 pound tofu, cubed
6 tablespoons popcorn flour
    cashew nuts

Soak the raisins in the juice for an hour or overnight.

In a food processor or blender, mix together the soaked raisins with the apple juice, tahini, vanilla, orange rind, honey, lemon juice, and tofu. Process until smooth.

Preheat oven to 350°F. Line 3 dozen minimuffin wells with foil or paper baking cups.

101

Put ½ teaspoon of popcorn flour in the bottom of each muffin cup, then spoon the batter on top of the flour. Place ½ cashew nut on top of each. Bake for 15 to 20 minutes.

Yield: 3 dozen minimuffins.

Approximately 22 calories each.

Popcorn Carob Cheesecake Muffins

Freeze these minimuffins, savor them slowly like an ice cream cone, and enjoy a nutritious sweet your waistline will love—only 33 calories each, including topping! Substitute 1 teaspoon vanilla-flavored whipped cream for the tofu topping, if you like, for the same calorie count.

1 egg
1 tablespoon honey
½ cup orange concentrate
1 teaspoon vanilla
½ cup cottage cheese
½ cup plumped raisins
1 cup popcorn flour*

¼ cup carob powder
2 tablespoons whole wheat
  pastry flour
2 teaspoons baking powder
½ teaspoon baking soda
1 teaspoon cinnamon

In a mixing bowl or food processor, blend the egg, honey, orange concentrate, vanilla, and cottage cheese. Stir in the raisins.

In another bowl, combine the popcorn flour, carob powder, whole wheat pastry flour, baking powder, baking soda, and cinnamon.

Line 24 minimuffin wells with paper liners. Preheat oven to 350°F.

Combine the two mixtures and mix briefly only to blend the ingredients.

Spoon the mixture into the muffin cups and bake for 15 minutes. Cool in pans for 10 minutes, then remove to a rack. When cool, top with maple tofu whip.

TOPPING

½ cup tofu	1 tablespoon Kahlúa (optional)
2 tablespoons maple syrup	1 tablespoon instant decaffein-
1 tablespoon orange	ated coffee crystals
concentrate	

To make the topping, blend together in a food processor or blender the tofu, maple syrup, orange concentrate, Kahlúa, and coffee.

When cool, frost the muffins. Place the frosted muffins on a tray and freeze. Serve them directly from the freezer.

Yield: 2 dozen minimuffins.

Approximately 33 calories each.

*1½ cups of popcorn whizzed in a coffee mill or seed grinder yield 1 cup of popcorn flour. Blenders and food processors do not grind the popcorn fine enough.

Heavenly Cheesecake Muffins

Indulge your yen for cheesecake without guilt. Each muffin has only 22 calories. You could add a dollop of unsweetened fruit conserve without endangering your waistline. Sorrell Ridge brand contains only 14 calories in a whole teaspoon.

8 ounces (1 cup) cottage
  cheese
2 eggs, separated
2 tablespoons whole wheat
  pastry flour

½ teaspoon vanilla
1 teaspoon lemon juice
1 teaspoon grated lemon rind
1 tablespoon honey

In a food processor, blend the cottage cheese until it is as smooth as cream. Add the egg yolks, pastry flour, vanilla, lemon juice, lemon rind, and honey and blend.

In another bowl, beat the egg whites until they stand in peaks.

Preheat oven to 300°F. Grease 24 minimuffin wells with a mixture of lecithin and oil or line with minimuffin paper baking cups.

Fold the egg whites into the cottage cheese mixture. Spoon the batter into the muffin wells and bake for 20 minutes.

Yield: 2 dozen minimuffins.
Approximately 22 calories each.

Light and Fluffy Cornmeal Muffins

Low-calorie popcorn flour adds flavor and a deliciously fluffy texture to these quick and easy muffins. Popcorn flour provides fiber, protein, and iron and is ridiculousy low in calories.

¼ cup sour cream	1½ cups popcorn flour*
¾ cup milk	2 tablespoons oat bran
⅓ cup maple syrup or ¼ cup honey	2 tablespoons wheat germ
2 eggs	½ teaspoon baking soda
¾ cup whole wheat pastry flour	sesame seeds

Preheat oven to 400°F. Grease 12 regular-size muffin wells with a lecithin and oil mixture, or line with paper or foil cups.

In a bowl or food processor, combine the sour cream, milk, maple syrup or honey, and eggs. Process to combine.

In another bowl, mix together the flours, oat bran, wheat germ, and baking soda. Combine the two mixtures and blend only until no flour is visible. Spoon into the prepared muffin cups. Top with sesame seeds. Bake for 15 minutes.

Yield: 12 muffins.

Approximately 85 calories each.

*1½ cups of popcorn whizzed in a coffee mill or seed grinder yield 1 cup of popcorn flour. Blenders and food processors do not grind the popcorn fine enough.

BLESS-YOUR-HEART MUFFINS

All the recipes in this book are extremely low in cholesterol. The recipes in this chapter, however, are loaded with ingredients that have been shown actually to *lower* cholesterol:

- Oat bran, according to nutritionist Jeffrey Bland, Ph.D., "is the best fiber supplement available for both lowering blood cholesterol and improving the management of blood sugar."
- Fruits, vegetables, whole grains, and legumes all have a beneficial effect on lowering blood cholesterol.
- Olive oil has been shown to lower the LDL (low-density lipoproteins) that are damaging to the arteries, without lowering the HDL (high-density lipoproteins) that are protective of the arteries. And in some instances olive oil actually increases HDL.
- Lecithin is a natural emulsifier that not only helps to keep your blood's cholesterol flowing freely, thus minimizing its tendency to form clots, but also has been shown in a recent study (at the Israel institute of Technology in Haifa) to lower LDL and increase HDL significantly. Lecithin was also shown to decrease triglyceride levels and to *inhibit platelet aggregation*. The optimal amount of lecithin supplementation ranges from 6 to 12 grams a day, according to the study.

Molasses is used as a sweetener in most of these muffins because of its high calcium and magnesium content. Both minerals are essential to the steady beat of your heart.

Spicy Bean Muffins

You won't believe how delicious a bean muffin can be! Beans are high in protein, low in calories, high in fiber, and contain no cholesterol. Pectin in the apple lowers cholesterol levels, and so does the oat bran. So enjoy in good health.

1 cup cooked, mashed pinto beans*	4 tablespoons oat bran
2 egg whites	2 tablespoons lecithin granules
3 tablespoons olive oil	½ teaspoon baking soda
1 teaspoon vanilla	½ teaspoon ground cinnamon
2 tablespoons molasses or honey	⅛ teaspoon ground nutmeg
½ cup sifted whole wheat pastry flour minus 2 tablespoons	⅛ teaspoon ground cloves
	1 cup diced apples
	½ cup raisins
	¼ cup chopped nuts

In a mixing bowl or food processor, combine the beans, egg whites, oil, vanilla, and molasses or honey.

In another bowl, combine the pastry flour, oat bran, lecithin granules, baking soda, and spices.

Preheat the oven to 350°F. Grease 12 regular-size muffin wells with a lecithin and oil mixture, or line with paper or foil cups.

Add the dry ingredients to the bean mixture and mix briefly to combine the ingredients. Stir in the apples, raisins, and nuts.

*1 cup of dried pinto beans will yield 2 cups cooked. The beans can be mashed with a little of the cooking water in your blender or food processor.

Spoon the batter into the muffin wells and bake for 20 minutes.
Yield: 12 muffins.
Approximately 110 calories each.

Blueberry Buttermilk Muffins

It's amazing that anything so good for you can taste so delicious. Blueberries provide vitamins A and C, potassium, calcium, iron, and manganese. The buttermilk (or yogurt) provides an acid medium that helps the body metabolize minerals. If you use frozen berries, add them in their frozen state to the dry ingredients, or the batter will turn blue.

2 egg whites, slightly beaten	1 tablespoon cinnamon
⅓ cup molasses	1 tablespoon grated orange rind
1 tablespoon olive oil	
¾ cup buttermilk or low-fat yogurt	1 teaspoon baking soda
	1 teaspoon baking powder
1 cup sifted whole wheat pastry flour	1½ cups blueberries
½ cup oat bran	walnuts and unsweetened blueberry conserve for
3 tablespoons lecithin granules	garnish (Sorrell Ridge is
2 tablespoons wheat germ	a good brand)

In a mixing bowl or food processor, blend together the egg whites, molasses, olive oil, and buttermilk or yogurt.

In another bowl, mix together the pastry flour, oat bran, lecithin granules, wheat germ, cinnamon, orange rind, baking soda, and baking powder.

Preheat oven to 400°F. Grease 12 regular-size muffin cups with a lecithin and oil mixture, or line with paper or foil baking cups.

Combine the 2 mixtures and mix just to moisten all the ingredients. Fold in the blueberries.

Spoon the batter into the muffin cups. Top each with ½ walnut and a dab of blueberry conserve. Bake for 15 to 20 minutes.
Yield: 12 muffins.
Approximately 125 calories each.

No-Egg Bran Apple Muffins

Here's a special treat for cholesterol-watchers. These eggless muffins are loaded with fiber, which has been shown to further lower cholesterol levels.

½ cup yogurt
½ cup wheat bran
1 cup whole wheat pastry
    flour
¼ cup wheat germ
¼ cup oat bran
½ cup rolled oats
2 teaspoons baking powder
1 teaspoon baking soda
½ teaspoon cinnamon

2 teaspoons grated orange
    rind
2 tablespoons oil
2 tablespoons molasses
2 large apples, shredded (2
    cups)
½ cup raisins, plumped
½ cup sunflower seeds
    walnuts or pecans as
    garnish

In a measuring cup or small bowl, combine the yogurt and wheat bran. Set aside. In a bowl, combine the pastry flour, wheat germ, oat bran, oats, baking powder, baking soda, cinnamon, and orange rind. Set aside.

In another bowl or food processor, combine the oil, molasses, shredded apples, plumped raisins, and the yogurt-wheat bran mixture. Process to combine.

Add the combined dry ingredients and the sunflower seeds and process only until the ingredients are well combined. Spoon into muffin tins that have been greased with a mixture of lecithin and oil. Top each one with ½ walnut or ½ pecan. Bake in preheated 350°F oven for about 25 to 30 minutes.

Yield: 12 large muffins.

Approximately 168 calories each.

Fruit 'n' Nut Oat Bran Muffins

Not only do these muffins contain no cholesterol and no concentrated sweetener, they also are rich in pectin, polyunsaturates, potassium, lecithin, and oat bran, which tend to lower cholesterol levels and enhance the health of the heart. As for your taste buds—they never had it so good.

1 apple, unpeeled, grated	3 tablespoons oat bran
1 cup raisins	2 tablespoons lecithin granules
1 cup chopped prunes	½ cup chopped almonds
1 cup chopped walnuts	3 egg whites, slightly beaten

In a mixing bowl, combine the apple, raisins, prunes, walnuts and almonds, oat bran, and lecithin granules. Add the egg whites, and mix to moisten the ingredients.

Preheat oven to 350°F. Line 3 dozen minimuffin cups with paper liners or grease with a mixture of lecithin and oil. Spoon the batter into the muffin cups and bake for 15 minutes.

Yield: 3 dozen minimuffins.

Approximately 55 calories each.

Sour Cream and Chive Muffins

The oat bran and lecithin in these muffins both tend to reduce cholesterol levels, making the sour cream in them more enjoyable. If you prefer, you can eliminate the sour cream and use 1 cup of yogurt. Serve them hot with yogurt creamless cheese.

½ cup sour cream
½ cup yogurt
1 clove garlic, minced
2 egg whites
2 tablespoons olive oil
1 tablespoon honey
1 cup sifted whole wheat
    pastry flour

2 tablespoons wheat germ
4 tablespoons oat bran
3 tablespoons lecithin granules
1 teaspoon baking powder
1 teaspoon baking soda
2 teaspoons chopped chives

In a small bowl, combine the sour cream, yogurt, and minced garlic. Set aside.

In a mixing bowl or food processor, mix together the egg whites, oil, honey, and sour cream mixture.

In another bowl, combine the pastry flour, wheat germ, oat bran, lecithin granules, baking powder, and baking soda.

Preheat oven to 400°F. Grease 12 regular-size muffin cups with an oil and lecithin mixture or line with foil baking cups.

Combine the wet and dry ingredients and mix only to combine (about 3 pulses of the food processor). Spoon the batter into the muffin cups, top with a sprinkle of chives, and bake for 20 minutes.
Yield: 12 muffins.

Approximately 108 calories each when made with ½ cup of sour cream, approximately 95 calories each when made with 1 cup of yogurt and no sour cream.

LIFE-OF-THE-PARTY MUFFINS

These very special party muffins are for those occasions when you really want to impress your family and friends with your muffin *savoir-faire*.

Some of these muffins could double as cupcakes. In fact, we have put several of them together in a circle, put a candle in each one, and then sung "Happy Birthday" to a blushing child. The child then takes over and, instead of struggling with a knife and cake crumbs, distributes the muffins to the celebrants.

The more sophisticated muffins—those made with liqueurs, for instance—add a very merry note to the more adult celebrations. Far better to serve liqueurs in muffins than in a glass. You won't have to worry about driving skills being impaired—the alcohol evaporates in the baking process. The flavor remains. So enjoy!

Mocha Kahlúa Cheesecake Muffins

These marvelous muffins are reminiscent of the cakes we enjoyed in Italy, where they have mastered the art of baking with liqueurs. They're perfect for dessert-and-coffee occasions at your house after a movie or the theater.

4 tablespoons cream cheese
2 tablespoons Kahlúa liqueur
2 tablespoons frozen orange
    concentrate
1 tablespoon honey
1 teaspoon vanilla
½ teaspoon cinnamon
2 eggs
¾ cup buttermilk
3 tablespoons vegetable or
    olive oil
3 tablespoons honey
1 tablespoon frozen orange
    concentrate

1 tablespoon instant coffee
    dissolved in 1 tablespoon
    boiling water
1 cup sifted whole wheat
    pastry flour
3 tablespoons carob powder
2 tablespoons wheat germ
1 teaspoon baking soda
1 teaspoon baking powder
½ cup raisins, plumped
½ cup chopped nuts or
    sunflower seeds
coconut and Bing cherries
    for garnish

In a small bowl or food processor, blend together the cream cheese, Kahlúa, orange concentrate, honey, vanilla, and cinnamon. Refrigerate.

In a large bowl or food processor, blend together the eggs, buttermilk, oil, honey, 1 tablespoon of orange concentrate, and 1 tablespoon of instant coffee dissolved in water. Combine this with the cheese mixture above.

In another bowl, mix together the pastry flour, carob powder, wheat germ, baking soda, and baking powder.

114

Preheat oven to 375°F. Grease 12 regular-size muffin cups with a mixture of lecithin and oil, or line with paper or foil baking cups. Combine the wet and dry ingredients. Stir in the raisins and nuts or sunflower seeds. Spoon mixture into muffin cups and garnish with coconut or Bing cherries.

Bake for 20 to 25 minutes or until a cake tester comes out clean. Let the muffins rest for 5 minutes, then remove to a rack to cool. **Yield:** 12 muffins.

Approximately 171 calories each.

Jack-o'-Lantern Muffins

Make these tasty muffins for Halloween and the kids will stay home! The pumpkin (a member of the squash family) provides calcium, phosphorus, potassium, iron, and a whopping 15,000 I.U. of vitamin A in every cup. Vitamin A improves your vision, keeps your skin healthy-looking, and increases your resistance to infection.

2 eggs
3 tablespoons honey
3 tablespoons olive or vegetable oil
1 tablespoon molasses
1 cup mashed pumpkin
1 cup sifted whole wheat pastry flour
2 tablespoons wheat germ
2 tablespoons oat bran

1 teaspoon baking powder
1 teaspoon baking soda
2 teaspoons cinnamon
¼ teaspoon nutmeg
¼ teaspoon ground cloves
1 tablespoon grated orange rind
½ cup raisins, plumped coconut or chopped nuts

CHEESE TOPPING

½ cup cottage cheese	½ teaspoon vanilla
4 tablespoons cream cheese	½ teaspoon lemon juice
2 tablespoons honey	

To make the topping, blend together the cottage cheese, cream cheese, honey, vanilla, and lemon juice in a blender or food processor until smooth.

To make the muffins, blend together in a mixing bowl or food processor the eggs, honey, oil, molasses, and pumpkin.

In another bowl, mix together the pastry flour, wheat germ, oat bran, baking powder, baking soda, cinnamon, nutmeg, cloves, and orange rind. Stir in the raisins.

Preheat oven to 400°F. Line 12 regular-size muffin wells with paper baking cups or grease with a mixture of lecithin and oil.

Mix together the pumpkin mixture and the dry ingredients. Put a tablespoon of batter in each muffin cup, then add a teaspoon of the topping. Top with the remaining batter. Bake for 20 to 25 minutes or until a cake tester comes out clean. Cool on a wire rack, then frost each muffin with the remaining cheese topping and garnish with coconut or chopped nuts.

Yield: 12 muffins.

Approximately 118 calories each without topping, approximately 142 calories each with topping, approximately 147 if you add coconut or chopped nuts.

Carob Banana Boat Muffins

If your kids are hooked on chocolate, try these delightful muffins. Make them ahead of a school trip or birthday party and store them in the freezer. They taste best when they're cold. Carob has the taste of chocolate without the oxalic acid, theobromine, and fat. Carob is high in potassium and low in calories.

1 large egg or 2 small eggs
2 tablespoons softened butter
   or olive oil
3 tablespoons honey or
   molasses
¾ cup mashed bananas (2
   small)
⅔ cup yogurt or buttermilk
1 teaspoon vanilla
1¼ cups whole wheat pastry
   flour
⅓ cup carob powder

2 tablespoons wheat germ
2 tablespoons oat bran
2 tablespoons wheat bran
2 teaspoons baking powder
1 teaspoon baking soda
1 tablespoon grated orange
   rind
1 teaspoon cinnamon
½ cup raisins, plumped
   walnuts and carob chips for
   garnish

In a mixing bowl or food processor, blend together the egg or eggs, butter or olive oil, honey or molasses, bananas, yogurt or buttermilk, and vanilla.

In another bowl, mix together the pastry flour, carob powder, wheat germ, oat bran, wheat bran, baking powder, baking soda, orange rind, and cinnamon.

Preheat oven to 400°F. Line 12 regular-size muffin wells with paper or foil baking cups, or grease with a mixture of lecithin and oil.

117

Combine the wet and dry mixtures and mix briefly, only until the dry ingredients are moistened. Stir in the raisins.

Spoon the batter into the muffin wells. Place ¼ walnut in the center of each, then place the carob chips in a circle around the walnut. Bake for 18 to 20 minutes.

Yield: 12 muffins.

Approximately 143 calories each.

Carob Mint Cashew Muffins

A lovely dessert muffin with a refreshing, minty flavor. Carob, also known as St. John's bread, could be said to be worth its weight in gold. In ancient times the seed of the carob was used as a standard by which to measure a carat of gold.

2 eggs
3 tablespoons olive or vegetable
   oil
3 tablespoons honey
1 tablespoon molasses
1 cup creamy carob mint tea
   (divided)*
1 cup sifted whole wheat
   pastry flour

½ cup carob powder
1 teaspoon baking powder
½ teaspoon baking soda
½ cup chopped cashews or
   walnuts
6 whole cashew nuts

*Creamy carob mint tea is available in most gourmet and health-food stores.

CAROB MINT TOPPING

¼ cup carob powder	½ cup creamy carob mint tea
2 tablespoons honey	2 drops peppermint extract

To make the topping, combine the carob powder, honey, and tea in a small saucepan. Bring to a boil, stirring constantly. Boil slowly for about 5 minutes. Remove from the heat, cool, and add the peppermint extract.

To make the muffins, blend together the eggs, oil, honey, molasses, and tea in a mixing bowl or food processor.

In another bowl, mix together the pastry flour, carob powder, baking powder, and baking soda.

Preheat oven to 400°F. Line 12 regular-size muffin wells with paper baking cups or grease with a mixture of lecithin and oil.

Combine the wet and dry mixtures and mix briefly, just enough to moisten the ingredients. Stir in the chopped nuts. Spoon 1 tablespoon of batter into each muffin well. Place about ½ teaspoon of carob mint topping on each, then distribute the rest of the batter, filling the muffin wells about ⅔ full. Top each with ½ cashew nut. Bake for 15 to 18 minutes or until nicely rounded and a cake tester comes out clean. Cool on a rack. Then swirl the rest of the carob mint topping around the cashew.

Yield: 12 muffins.

Approximately 166 calories each.

SMART MUFFINS FOR THE ALLERGIC

If any members of your family are allergic to cow's milk, wheat, corn, chocolate, or eggs, they can still enjoy muffins. The recipes in this chapter have been devised to bypass one or more of these common allergens.

In addition, you can adapt any recipe from the rest of the book by following the guidelines on pages 25–28.

Dynamite Millet Raisin Muffins

Millet is one of the most nutritious and well balanced of all the grains. It is also the least allergenic and is easy to digest. It is very high in protein, the vitamin B's, lecithin, and minerals. Its high mineral content makes it an alkaline food. Other grains have an acid reaction. Millet is considered an outstanding antacid food, well tolerated by ulcer and colitis patients.

1 cup raisins	2 tablespoons rice polish
¾ cup fruit juice or water	2 tablespoons soy flour
1 egg	2 teaspoons baking powder
1 cup buttermilk, yogurt, or sour milk	1 teaspoon baking soda
2 tablespoons honey	1 teaspoon cinnamon
1 tablespoon molasses	1 tablespoon grated orange rind
1 cup millet flour	pinch of ground cloves
1 cup uncooked rolled oats	pinch of ginger
2 tablespoons oat bran	½ cup sunflower seeds

In a saucepan, combine the raisins and fruit juice or water, bring to a boil, then simmer for 5 minutes. Set aside to cool.

In a mixing bowl or food processor, blend together the egg, buttermilk or yogurt, or sour milk, honey, and molasses.

In another bowl, mix together the flour, oats, oat bran, rice polish, soy flour, baking powder, baking soda, cinnamon, orange rind, cloves, and ginger.

Preheat oven to 400°F. Line 12 muffin wells with paper liners or grease with a mixture of lecithin and oil.

Add the cooled raisin mixture to the liquid ingredients, then add the dry ingredients and mix briefly only until the ingredients are well combined. Stir in the sunflower seeds.

Fill the muffin wells with the batter and bake for 25 minutes or until the tops are well rounded and golden and a cake tester or wooden pick inserted in the center comes out clean.

Yield: 12 muffins.

Approximately 115 calories each.

Buckwheat Pumpkin Spice Muffins

Use white buckwheat flour for a mild and mellow flavor. It's made from unroasted whole groats. These muffins are moist, tender, and flavorful if you don't overbake them. Buckwheat muffins tend to dry out quickly if cooked too long.

2 eggs
¾ cup mashed, cooked pumpkin
2 tablespoons olive or vegetable oil
⅔ cup milk or fruit juice
2 tablespoons honey
1 tablespoon molasses
1 cup buckwheat flour
¼ cup soy flour
1 tablespoon baking powder

1 teaspoon baking soda
1 teaspoon cinnamon
1 tablespoon grated orange rind
½ teaspoon ginger
¼ teaspoon ground cloves
⅛ teaspoon freshly grated nutmeg
½ cup raisins

In a mixing bowl or food processor, blend together the eggs, pumpkin, oil, milk or fruit juice, honey, and molasses.

In another bowl, mix together the flours, baking powder, baking soda, spices, and raisins.

Preheat oven to 400°F. Grease 12 regular-size muffin cups with a lecithin and oil mixture or line with foil baking cups. Bake for 15 to 20 minutes or until a cake tester comes out clean.

Yield: 12 muffins.

Approximately 113 calories each.

Rye, Rice, and Raisin Muffins

Crisp tops, a tender crumb, and a marvelous fragrance make these *wheat-free* muffins very popular, even among those who can handle wheat. The wheat polish in these muffins is an excellent source of the B vitamin niacin, which reduces blood cholesterol levels and contributes to mental and emotional health.

2 eggs
2 tablespoons molasses
1 tablespoon honey
2 tablespoons olive oil
1 cup yogurt or buttermilk
1¾ cups rye flour
¼ cup rice polish
3 tablespoons lecithin granules
3 tablespoons oat bran

1 teaspoon baking powder
½ teaspoon baking soda
1 tablespoon grated orange rind
1 teaspoon cinnamon
¼ teaspoon ground cloves
¼ teaspoon ground nutmeg
½ cup raisins, plumped
½ cup sunflower seeds

In a mixing bowl or food processor, blend together the eggs, molasses, honey, olive oil, and yogurt or buttermilk.

In another bowl, mix together the rye flour, rice polish, lecithin granules, oat bran, baking powder, baking soda, orange rind, cinnamon, cloves, and nutmeg.

Preheat oven to 400°F. Line 12 regular-size muffin wells with paper or foil baking cups, or grease with lecithin and oil.

Combine the two mixtures, then stir in the raisins and seeds. Spoon the batter into the muffin wells and bake for 12 to 15 minutes or until a cake tester comes out clean.

Yield: 12 muffins.

Approximately 143 calories each.

Tofu Bran Blueberry Eggless Muffins

High-protein, high-fiber, low-calorie, no cholesterol—these muffins provide a nutritional bonanza especially valuable to those who cannot eat eggs. They're great as an afternoon pickup or late-night snack.

½ cup wheat bran
1 cup buttermilk, sour milk, or yogurt
½ cup drained, mashed tofu
2 tablespoons olive or vegetable oil
3 tablespoons honey
¾ cup applesauce
½ cup wheat sprouts (optional)
1 cup sifted whole wheat pastry flour
¼ cup oat bran

2 tablespoons lecithin granules
1 teaspoon baking soda
1 teaspoon baking powder
1 tablespoon grated orange rind
½ teaspoon cinnamon grating of whole nutmeg
¼ teaspoon allspice
1½ to 2 cups blueberries
½ cup sunflower seeds orange marmalade for garnish

In a small bowl, combine the wheat bran and buttermilk, sour milk, or yogurt. In another small bowl or food processor, blend together the tofu, oil, honey, and applesauce. Add the bran mixture and the wheat sprouts.

In another bowl, combine the pastry flour, oat bran, lecithin granules, baking soda, baking powder, orange rind, cinnamon, nutmeg, and allspice. Stir in the blueberries.

Preheat oven to 375°F. Grease 12 muffin wells with a lecithin and oil mixture, or line with foil or paper cups.

Combine the two mixtures gently, trying not to break the blueberries. Fold in the sunflower seeds.

Spoon the batter into the muffin wells, and top each with a dab of orange marmalade (Sorrell Ridge unsweetened or your own).

Bake for 25 minutes or until toasty brown and a toothpick inserted in the center comes out clean.

Yield: 12 large muffins.

Approximately 116 calories each.

Maple Pecan Rye and Millet Muffins

A very nice consistency, a tender crumb, and a lovely maple flavor. The rye flour in these delicious muffins provides body-building protein, high-energy complex carbohydrates, and a hearty flavor that marries well the mild flavor and high mineral content of the millet flour.

2 large eggs
3 tablespoons olive or vegetable oil
⅓ cup maple syrup
¾ cup orange or apple juice
1 cup millet flour

1 cup rye flour
1 teaspoon baking soda
1 teaspoon baking powder
½ cup chopped pecans or walnuts
pecans for garnish

In a mixing bowl or food processor, blend together the eggs, oil, maple syrup, and juice.

In another bowl, mix together the flours, baking soda, and baking powder.

Preheat oven to 400°F. Line 12 regular-size muffin wells with paper or foil baking cups, or grease with a mixture of lecithin and oil.

Combine the wet and dry ingredients and blend only until the ingredients are well blended. Stir in the chopped nuts.

Spoon the batter into the muffin wells. Top each with a pecan nugget and bake for 18 to 20 minutes or until a cake tester comes out clean.

Yield: 12 muffins.

Approximately 152 calories each.

Pumpernickel Currant Muffins

These muffins make music in your mouth and in your arteries. Currants are a good source of omega 3 and omega 6 fatty acids, both of which enhance your chances of avoiding a heart attack or stroke by reducing cholesterol and triglycerides. I developed these muffins for my granddaughter who is allergic to wheat, but everybody is gobbling them up!

2 eggs
3 tablespoons olive or vegetable oil
4 tablespoons molasses
1 cup yogurt
1 cup rye flour
¼ cup brown rice flour
2 tablespoons carob powder
¼ cup cornmeal
2 tablespoons lecithin granules
2 tablespoons oat bran

1 teaspoon baking soda
1 teaspoon baking powder
½ teaspoon cinnamon
¼ teaspoon cloves
¼ teaspoon allspice
1 tablespoon grated orange rind
¾ cup currants
½ cup roasted chopped filberts filbert halves for garnish

In a mixing bowl or food processor, blend together the eggs, oil, molasses, and yogurt.

In another bowl, combine the flours, carob powder, cornmeal, lecithin granules, oat bran, baking soda, baking powder, and the spices.

Preheat oven to 375°F. Line 12 regular-size muffin wells with baking cups or grease with a mixture of oil and lecithin.

Combine the wet and dry mixtures and mix briefly, just to combine. Stir in the currants and the chopped filberts. Spoon the mixture into the muffin wells, top each with a filbert, and bake for about 20 minutes.

Yield: 12 muffins.

Approximately 177 calories each.

Brown Rice Hazelnut Muffins

These three-flour muffins have amino acids that complement each other; thus they provide protein of high biological value. They are incredibly delicious when served with yogurt cheese and apple butter.

2 eggs
3 tablespoons olive or vegetable oil
3 tablespoons honey
1 teaspoon vanilla
⅔ cup buttermilk, yogurt, or sour milk
½ cup cooked brown rice
½ cup plumped raisins

2 tablespoons millet, soy, or rice flour
⅔ cup rye flour
½ cup chick-pea flour
2 teaspoons baking powder
1 teaspoon baking soda
½ teaspoon cinnamon
¼ teaspoon nutmeg
12 hazelnuts

In a mixing bowl or food processor, blend together the eggs, oil, honey, vanilla, and buttermilk, yogurt, or sour milk. Stir in the rice and the plumped and cooled raisins.

In another bowl, combine the flours, baking powder, baking soda, cinnamon, and nutmeg.

Preheat oven to 400°F. Line 12 regular-size muffin wells with baking cups or grease with a mixture of lecithin and oil.

Combine the wet and dry ingredients and stir only enough to moisten. Spoon the batter into the muffin wells, top each muffin with a hazelnut, and bake for 15 to 20 minutes or until the tops are brown and rounded and a cake tester comes out clean.
Yield: 12 muffins.
Approximately 146 calories each.

Raw Fruit Muffins

These are hypoallergenic dreams—*no wheat, no eggs, no dairy*—but what a lot of nutrition they deliver! Raw foods provide many important enzymes that are zapped by heat. The blend of nuts, seeds, and fruit provides iron, calcium, magnesium, and many valuable trace minerals that, in small amounts, play an essential role in the body.

½ cup pitted dates
½ cup dried figs
½ cup raisins
½ cup sunflower seeds
½ cup chopped almonds
¼ cup chopped pecans or
    walnuts
1 tablespoon grated orange
    rind
1 teaspoon grated lemon rind

½ cup unsweetened coconut
1 chopped apple
2 tablespoons honey
¼ cup orange juice
2 teaspoons lemon juice
2 tablespoons Amaretto,
    brandy, or apple juice
½ teaspoon cinnamon
½ teaspoon nutmeg
sesame seeds

Combine all the ingredients except the sesame seed in a blender or food processor. Line 24 minimuffin wells with paper liners. Form the batter into walnut-size balls, roll each one in sesame seeds, and place in the muffin cups. No need to bake these muffins—they're ready to eat, or can be stored in your freezer.

Yield: 24 minifruitcakes.

Approximately 86 calories each.

Steamed Raisin Muffins

When you don't want to use the oven, use a steamer and make these moist, puddinglike muffins. This recipe calls for rye flour, but you could substitute whatever kind meets your family's taste and allergy requirements. For the raisins, you could substitute currants, prunes, or apricots.

2 eggs
2 tablespoons olive oil or melted butter
2 tablespoons honey or molasses
½ cup milk or fruit juice
½ cup rye flour

¼ cup wheat bran
¼ cup oat bran
2 teaspoons baking powder
1 teaspoon cinnamon
1 tablespoon grated orange rind
½ raisins

In a mixing bowl or food processor, blend the eggs, olive oil or butter, honey or molasses, and milk or fruit juice.

In another bowl, combine the flour, wheat and oat bran, baking powder, cinnamon, and orange rind.

Combine the wet and dry ingredients, then stir in the raisins. Spoon the batter into 6 buttered custard cups and let steam for 35 minutes. Very good with vanilla sauce (see the recipe on page 143).

Yield: 6 muffins.

Approximately 150 calories each.

EXOTIC MUFFINS

This section includes muffins that contain unorthodox ingredients you don't usually associate with muffins. They can be served for an infinite variety of occasions. They're wholesome, flavorful, and adapt well to fancy dessert tray, lunch box, or brown bag.

The Popovers, when stuffed with tuna or salmon salad, give pizzazz to an everyday dish. They can also be stuffed with ice cream, whipped cream, or custard for an elegant dessert.

The Pumpkin Peach Chutney Muffins have a character all their own, quite different form the usual muffin. You probably wouldn't want them for breakfast, but they do elevate a lunch or dinner to gourmet status.

The Happy New Year Honey Cake Muffins with Kahlúa or Amaretto get the new year going on a heady note, and you simply must try the Powerhouse Carrot Coconut Muffins. They've got so much going for them, they could meet the standards set by every category of muffin in this book.

Pumpkin Peach Chutney Muffins

These muffins have an appealing, spunky flavor. Serve them warm with yogurt cream cheese and additional chutney, a tangy, sweet-and-sour condiment made with fruits, nuts, and spices.

2 large eggs
2 tablespoons olive, walnut,
   or vegetable oil
2 tablespoons honey
½ cup buttermilk or yogurt
1 cup puréed pumpkin
2 tablespoons wheat bran
¾ cup peach chutney (see the
   following recipe)
1½ cups whole wheat pastry
   flour

2 tablespoons wheat germ
2 tablespoons oat bran
2 tablespoons lecithin granules
1 teaspoon baking soda
1 teaspoon baking powder
1½ teaspoons cinnamon
¼ teaspoon freshly grated
   nutmeg
⅛ teaspoon allspice
1 teaspoon grated orange rind

In a mixing bowl or food processor, blend together the eggs, oil, honey, buttermilk or yogurt, pumpkin, wheat bran, and chutney.

In another bowl, mix together the pastry flour, wheat germ, oat bran, lecithin granules, baking soda, baking powder, cinnamon, nutmeg, allspice, and orange rind.

Preheat oven to 400°F. Line 12 regular-size muffin wells with baking cups, or grease with a mixture of lecithin and oil.

Combine the wet and dry ingredients and stir the mixture until just combined. Spoon the batter into the muffin wells and bake for about 20 minutes or until a tester comes out clean.
Yield: 12 muffins.
Approximately 111 calories each.

Peach Chutney

1¼ cups sliced peaches
3 tablespoons honey
1½ tablespoons apple cider,
    raspberry or wine vinegar
¾ teaspoon minced, peeled
    ginger root or ½
    teaspoon ground ginger

½ cup raw cashews, coarsely
    chopped
½ cup raisins

In a small bowl, combine the peaches, honey, vinegar, and ginger and mix well. Stir in the cashews and raisins and mix again.
Yield: about 2¼ cups.
Approximately 25 calories in 1 tablespoon.
Variation: Use apricot, pear, or apple for the chutney.

Happy New Year Honey Cake Muffins

We serve these miniature honey cakes with sliced apples to symbolize our wish for a sweet and fruitful year. We use apricots, which are very rich in blood-building iron, and walnuts, a good source of omega 3 fatty acids, to help make it a year of good health.

4 large eggs
2 tablespoons olive oil, walnut oil, or vegetable oil
½ cup honey
½ cup fruit juice or herbal tea
3 tablespoons applesauce
2 tablespoons brandy, Kahlúa, or Amaretto liqueur
3 cups sifted whole wheat pastry flour
3 tablespoons lecithin granules
3 tablespoons oat bran
2 tablespoons wheat germ
3 tablespoons soy flour or powder

½ teaspoon allspice
1 teaspoon ground cloves
½ teaspoon cinnamon
1 teaspoon baking soda
1½ teaspoons baking powder
1 cup raisins
12 dried apricots, chopped or diced
½ cup chopped walnuts
orange or orange cherry marmalade, unsweetened (Sorrell Ridge is good)
sliced or chopped almonds for garnish

In a large mixing bowl or food processor, blend together the eggs, oil, honey, fruit juice or herbal tea, applesauce, and brandy or liqueur.

In another bowl, mix together the pastry flour, lecithin granules, oat bran, wheat germ, soy flour or powder, spices, baking soda, and baking powder.

135

Preheat oven to 350°F. Grease 18 regular-size muffin wells with a lecithin and oil mixture, or line with foil or paper cups.

Combine the wet and dry ingredients and mix only until well blended. Stir in the raisins, apricots, and walnuts. Half fill the muffin wells with batter. Spoon a teaspoon of conserve on each one, then divide the remaining batter among the muffins. Top each with a few almond slices or chopped almonds.

Bake for 20 to 25 minutes or until a cake tester comes out clean.
Yield: 18 muffins.
Approximately 190 calories each.

Powerhouse Carrot Coconut Muffins

These muffins are exceptionally high in protein, fiber, and beta carotene—shown to be an effective antioxidant that helps to hold back the aging process and retard the development of malignancies. You could make a meal out of one with a salad and be very well nourished.

¾ cup hot water
½ cup raisins
2 carrots, grated (about 1 cup)
2 large eggs
2 tablespoons molasses
1 tablespoon honey
2 tablespoons olive or vegetable oil
2 tablespoons wheat bran
1¼ cups sifted whole wheat pastry flour
¼ cup rice polish
3 tablespoons oat bran

¼ cup lecithin granules
¼ cup dry milk powder
3 tablespoons sesame seeds
1 tablespoon nutritional yeast
1 teaspoon kelp
1 teaspoon baking soda
2 teaspoons baking powder
1½ teaspoons cinnamon
¼ teaspoon ground nutmeg
¼ teaspoon allspice
1 tablespoon grated orange rind
½ cup chopped walnuts
¼ cup flaked coconut

In a small bowl, soak the raisins in the hot water. Set aside.

In a mixing bowl or food processor, grate the carrots and blend with the eggs, molasses, honey, and oil. Mix in the wheat bran, and the water the raisins were soaked in.

In another bowl, mix together the pastry flour, rice polish, oat bran, lecithin granules, milk powder, sesame seeds, nutritional yeast, kelp, baking soda, baking powder, cinnamon, nutmeg, allspice, and orange rind.

Preheat oven to 400°F. Line 12 regular-size muffin wells with baking cups or grease with a mixture of lecithin and oil.

Combine the wet and dry mixtures and mix just until the ingredients are combined. Fold in the raisins, walnuts, and coconut. Spoon into the muffin cups and bake for about 20 minutes or until a cake tester comes out dry.

Yield: 12 muffins.

Approximately 182 calories each.

Popovers

These are shiny, crisp containers for tuna or salmon salad, or for elegant lemon custard or Bavarian cream fillings.

3 eggs	¾ cup whole wheat pastry flour
1 cup milk	2 tablespoons wheat germ
2 tablespoons olive or vegetable oil	2 tablespoons oat bran
	2 tablespoons soy flour

Preheat oven to 375°F.

In a medium-size mixing bowl, using an electric beater, beat the eggs until foamy. Continue to beat as you add the milk and oil, then the pastry flour combined with the wheat germ, oat bran, and soy flour.

Grease 12 regular-size muffin wells with a lecithin and oil mixture.

Spoon the batter into the muffin wells till they are about ⅔ full. Bake for 40 to 50 minutes until golden brown and puffed up like tennis balls.

Yield: 12 popovers.

Approximately 78 calories each.

Variation: Sprinkle grated cheese on 1 tablespoon of the batter in each muffin well, then top with the rest of the batter.

Whole Wheat Cinnamon Raisin
English Muffins

Split these muffins with a fork and toast the cut sides. Serve with yogurt cheese and fruit conserve.

1 tablespoon dry yeast	3¼ cups whole wheat bread flour
¼ cup warm water	¼ cup wheat germ
1 teaspoon honey	1½ teaspoons cinnamon
1¾ cups warm milk	½ cup raisins

In a small bowl, dissolve the yeast in the water and add the honey. Set aside to proof for 10 minutes.

In a larger bowl, combine the milk, bread flour, wheat germ, and cinnamon. Add the yeast mixture and raisins and beat well.

Cover and let rise in a warm place until double in bulk (about 1 hour).

Heat a heavy griddle, skillet, or baking sheet on top of the stove. Brush with oil. Grease several crumpet rings, small tuna cans with both ends removed, or canning jar rings. Keep the heat under the griddle low.

With a spoon or ladle, half fill the rings. Cook the muffins about 6 minutes on each side or until brown on both sides.

Yield: 15 muffins.

Approximately 157 calories each.

SMART TOPPINGS FOR SMART MUFFINS

Toppings can add moistness and flavor to your muffins. In making your choice, consider these calorie counts:

Butter: 100 calories in 1 tablespoon
Sour cream: 475 calories per cup
Yogurt (whole milk): 152 calories per cup
Yogurt (partially skimmed milk): 123 calories per cup
Cream cheese: 100 calories per ounce
Cottage cheese (4.2 percent milk fat): 30 calories per ounce
Yogurt cream cheese (from whole milk yogurt): 40 calories per ounce
Yogurt cream cheese (made from partially skimmed milk yogurt): 38 calories per ounce
Tofu: 21½ calories per ounce

These toppings should be added on before baking: a sprinkling of rolled oats, poppy seeds, sunflower seeds, chopped peanuts, chopped almonds, almond slices, and walnut, pecan, and cashew halves.

The following toppings should be applied after the muffins are baked and cooled:

Yogurt Creamless Cheese

This spread has a pleasant tang and is low in calories.

Place 1 pint of plain yogurt in a colander lined with 3 layers of cheesecloth, a cheese bag, or a clean tea towel. Let it drain into a bowl for several hours or overnight. In the morning you will have 6 ounces of wonderful yogurt cheese. The liquid that has drained into the bowl is whey and can be used in soup or in baking.

The yogurt cheese can be spread plain on muffins or mixed with fruit conserve, nuts, spices, or flavorings.

Yield: 6 ounces.

Approximately 20 calories per tablespoon.

Apricot Almond Jam

½ cup dried apricots   apple juice to cover
6 whole almonds   1 teaspoon grated orange rind
½ cup raisins

Combine the apricots, almonds, and raisins in a jar. Cover with the apple juice. Let stand overnight in the refrigerator.

Whiz the soaked apricots, almonds, raisins, the residual apple juice, and the orange rind in a food processor or blender.

Yield: 1 cup.

Approximately 8½ calories in a teaspoon.

Vanilla Sauce

2 tablespoons butter
2 tablespoons whole wheat
    pastry flour

1 cup boiling water
2 tablespoons honey
1 teaspoon vanilla

In a saucepan, melt the butter, add the pastry flour, and stir until it bubbles. Add the boiling water and honey. Bring to a boil and cook for about 10 minutes. Add the vanilla.
Yield: about ⅔ cup.
Approximately 32 calories in a tablespoon.

Fig, Raisin, and Nut Spread

½ cup figs, diced
½ cup raisins
½ cup hazelnuts or skinned
    peanuts

1 tablespoon orange marma-
    lade, unsweetened

Combine the figs and raisins in a bowl or food processor, using a steel blade. Process to a smooth consistency. Add the nuts, and process until they are finely chopped. Stir in the orange marmalade. Spread on hot muffins.

If you have any of this spread left over, form into balls and roll in coconut or sesame seeds. Makes a delicious confection.
Yield: 1½ cups.
Approximately 12 calories in a teaspoon.

Banana Peanut Butter Delight

2 medium bananas
2–3 tablespoons honey or
 molasses

¼ cup yogurt
¼ teaspoon cinnamon
½ cup peanut butter

In a flat bowl or food processor, blend all the ingredients until smooth.
Yield: about 1 cup.
Approximately 22 calories in a teaspoon.
  This topping also makes delicious Popsicles. Just spoon into 3-ounce paper cups, insert Popsicle sticks, and freeze. Or top with crushed nuts and carob syrup to make darling little miniature sundaes. Let thaw a few minutes before slurping.

Banana Cottage Cheese Topping

A substantial topping that doubles as a dessert pudding.

½ cup cottage cheese
1 banana
½ teaspoon cinnamon

2 teaspoons unsweetened
 orange marmalade (Sor-
 rell Ridge)

In a flat bowl or food processor, blend all the ingredients together until smooth.
Yield: about ½ cup.
Approximately 17 calories in a tablespoon.

MAKE YOUR OWN
BREADS AND BISCUITS

If you have never baked a loaf of bread, you have missed out on one of life's elemental joys. There is nothing like it.

Not even winning an Oscar or getting an income tax rebate could put you on cloud nine like watching your family and guests devour beautiful biscuits and breads that you have conjured up with the help of your oven, a little yeast, flour, and sundry ingredients designed by Nature to put a healthy glow on body and spirit.

Bread baking was once a routine household procedure incumbent on every proper housewife. Today it is considered a hobby for men and women alike.

As if the heady fragrance that fills the house weren't enough of an inducement, there is the kneading process that many bread bakers consider a form of therapy.

I agree with Betty Iams, who said in her booklet "Bread Baking from A to Z" (Clef House Publications, Temecula, California), "There is no other hobby in the world as rewarding as bread baking. When you are happy, it is a joy to breeze though the kneading process. When you are sad, frustrated, unhappy, you can unleash all your hostilities on the helpless dough as you knead away. Whatever your state of mind, the bread-making process is sure to have an uplifting effect."

In case you have no aggressions, it's still great exercise and a good slimmer for the upper arms.

And, of course, baking your own breads is good for the budget and wonderful for your well-being. You get two beautiful, nutritious, chemical-free loaves of home-baked bread for what it costs for one mediocre loaf (with questionable additives) at market prices.

The recipes that follow will guide you toward bread-baking heaven every step of the way.

Hi-Fiber Wheat and Soy Quick Bread

A delicious crusty bread that keeps you moving. Each slice provides a tablespoon of wonder-working bran. The soy enhances its antioxidant value.

¾ cup whole wheat pastry flour
¼ cup soy flour
1½ cups coarse bran
1 tablespoon baking powder
½ teaspoon cinnamon
¼ teaspoon ginger
¼ teaspoon freshly grated nutmeg

1 teaspoon grated orange rind
1 cup plain yogurt
2 tablespoons vegetable oil
1 egg
¼ cup honey or unsulphured molasses

Heat oven to 350°F.

In a large bowl, combine the flours, bran, baking powder, cinnamon, ginger, nutmeg, and orange rind. Stir to blend.

In a food processor or mixing machine, blend together the yogurt, oil, egg, and honey or molasses. Add the dry ingredients and process only until ingredients are blended.

Turn the batter into an 8 × 4-inch loaf pan spritzed with baking spray. Bake for 40 to 45 minutes or until a cake tester comes out clean. Allow to cool for about 10 minutes, then invert on a wire rack to cool completely. Scrumptious with cream cheese, peanut butter, or jelly.

Yield: Makes 1 loaf, 12 slices. *Each slice provides 100 calories.*

Variations:

This batter would make 12 delicious muffins. Bake for 20 to 25 minutes.

Vary the pleasure of the loaf or muffins by adding raisins or currants, sunflower seeds, or walnuts to the dry ingredients before combining with the liquid ingredients.

146

Yeast-Risen Staff-of-Life Bread

A couple of slices of this high-protein loaf really hits the spot on long trips, picnics, and in your pocket or handbag on mornings when you oversleep and have no time for breakfast.

1 cup warm water
2 tablespoons blackstrap
    molasses
2 tablespoons baking yeast
2 cups whole wheat bread flour
½ cup soy flour
3 tablespoons wheat germ
3 tablespoons oat bran

4 tablespoons spray dried
    powdered milk
1½ teaspoons salt-free herbal
    seasoner
¼ cup millet
¼ cup nutritional yeast
¼ cup wheat bran pre-soaked in
    ½ cup warm water

Heat oven to 400°F.

Put the warm water in a bowl and add the molasses, then the yeast.

In another bowl, combine the flours, wheat germ, milk powder, herbal seasoner, and millet. Add this mixture of dry ingredients to the yeast mixture. Add the soaked bran with its liquid. If necessary, add a little more flour to make a soft dough. Knead for about 5 minutes.

Place the dough in an oiled bowl. Cover and place in a warm area to rise for about 2 hours. Punch the dough down and let it rise again for 20 minutes. Form into 2 small loaves and let it rise in a warm place until it doubles in bulk.

Bake for 10 minutes, then lower the oven to 350°F and bake for 50 minutes or until it makes a hollow sound when you thump it.

Yield: Makes 2 loaves, 16 slices apiece. *Each slice provides 55 calories.*

High-Protein Granola Bread

Even the breakfast-skippers in your family will make time for a slice or two of toasted granola bread in the morning. It's a high-octane boost and irresistibly delicious.

2½ tablespoons dry baking yeast
½ cup warm water
1 egg
¼ cup honey or maple syrup
¼ cup unsalted butter, softened
1 cup milk, scalded
2 cups granola
½ cup wheat germ

1 tablespoon grated orange rind
3½ cups whole wheat bread flour
½ cup soy flour
1 egg yolk
1 teaspoon water
½ cup chopped walnuts
1 teaspoon cinnamon

Dissolve the yeast in the warm water and let it stand until it bubbles.

In a large bowl, combine the egg, honey or maple syrup, butter, and milk. Stir in the granola and wheat germ, orange rind, and the yeast mixture.

Combine the wheat and soy flours and add gradually to the yeast mixture to form a dough. On a floured surface, knead the dough for about 10 minutes. Place the dough in a greased bowl. Brush surface of dough with oil or melted butter. Cover and let rise in a warm place until double in bulk, about 2 hours.

Punch dough down, knead briefly, then divide into 2 equal portions. Shape each half into a loaf and place each in a greased loaf pan 8 × 4 × 2½ inches. Let the dough rise again for about an hour or until the sides of the dough reach the top of the pans and the dough doubles in bulk. Brush the tops with egg wash made by combining the egg yolk with the

148

teaspoon of water. Sprinkle with a mixture of the chopped nuts and cinnamon.

Bake in a preheated 350°F oven for about 50 minutes.

Yield: Makes 2 deliciously fragrant loaves, 16 slices each loaf. *Each slice provides 77 calories.*

Sourdough Starter

½ cup lukewarm water
1 teaspoon yeast (a natural
    leavening such as "Lacto
    Leven Lifter" is good—

may be ordered by mail
from Oscar Theirson,
Juda, Wisc.)

Soak 5 minutes.

Add: ½ cup warm water and enough rye flour (or other whole grain flour) to make a soft batter.

Place in bowl large enough to allow mixture to double in bulk.

Cover lightly and set at room temperature. Do not stir, but let rise and fall for 24 to 36 hours, depending on sourness desired. If you do not use at once, cover tightly and refrigerate.

Simple Sour Rye Bread

8 cups fresh whole rye flour
3 cups warm water

½ cup sourdough starter

Mix 7 cups of flour with water and sourdough starter. Cover and let stand in warm place overnight. Add remaining flour and mix well. Place in oiled pans. Let rise for about a half hour. Bake at 350°F. for about one

hour. Be sure to retain a half cup of dough as a starter for your next baking. Keep it in a tightly closed jar in the refrigerator.
Yield: Makes 2 large loaves, 18 slices apiece. *Each slice provides 52 calories.*

Rye Bread

Place 2 level tablespoons yeast in a cup of warm water. Set aside. In mixing bowl place:

2 *cups whole wheat flour*	2 *eggs*
1 *cup rye flour*	½ *cup oil*
2 *cups warm water*	
½ *cup molasses and honey mixed*	
½ *cup powdered milk (not instant)*	

Beat a few seconds with electric beater; add yeast.

Cover bowl with towel. Set aside in warm place until doubled in bulk.

Add 1 tablespoon sea salt and 4 tablespoons caraway seeds.

Measure 3 cups rye flour. Gradually add flour to mixture until it can be handled on board without excessive sticking. Knead in remaining flour. Rye flour dough is very sticky, so moisten hands now and then with any vegetable oil. Knead well, then shape into 2 loaves.

Place into two oiled pans. When almost doubled in bulk, or when dough does not spring back when lightly pressed with finger, place in oven preheated to 350°F. Bake for 45 minutes.

Turn out on rack to cool.

Yield: Makes 2 loaves, 20 slices each. *Each slice provides 60 calories.*

Corn Bread (Sourdough Rye)

Funny thing about this Corn Bread—it's made from rye and wheat flours. There is cornmeal on the bottom of the loaf, but none at all in the loaf itself. There is no similarity in taste, texture, or nutritional content to the corn muffins or cornmeal bread generally available in America. This is a European bread. In Europe, the word for corn is maize, and there "corn" means grain—any grain.

In New England, this bread is called sitzell and is served in a little Cambridge restaurant frequented by students from Harvard and MIT.

You must plan ahead when you make this bread, but it's worth it. The bread itself is made in two stages, but first you must prepare a rye sourdough starter.

RYE SOURDOUGH STARTER

1 package dry yeast
2 cups warm water
2 cups rye flour

1 small onion, peeled and
    speared through several
    times with a fork

Dissolve the yeast in the warm water. Add the flour and stir. Add the onion. Place the mixture in a large (2 quarts or more) glass or crockery pot with a lid and cover loosely. Let stand at room temperature overnight. In the morning, remove the onion. Continue to let the mixture stand at room temperature for a day or 2, until it develops a nice "fermented" smell. Then it is ready to use. If the mixture separates, that is normal; just stir before using.

To keep the sourdough starter going, just add water and rye flour in equal parts (1 cup of each) to bring the pot back to its original level. If the yeast in a sourdough starter is to remain active, it occasionally has to be

151

"fed" with new flour. So, use your pot at least once a week, preferably twice, which isn't hard to do. In between, keep the pot covered and refrigerated.

If you haven't used your sourdough pot for a while and the starter doesn't bubble up within a reasonable period of time (several hours) after adding new flour and water to it, you can help it along by adding a little yeast—about 1 tablespoon.

Now, to make the actual bread.

STAGE ONE: THE NIGHT BEFORE

1 *cup rye sourdough starter*
1½ *cups warm water*
3 *cups medium rye flour*
1 *small onion, peeled and* *speared through several times with a fork (optional)*

Stir these ingredients together in a bowl; cover, and let sit overnight. The onion is optional, but it gives added acidity and a certain subtle flavor to the bread.

STAGE TWO: THE NEXT MORNING

1 *package dry baking yeast*
½ *cup warm water*
1 *tablespoon salt*
1 *tablespoon caraway seeds*
1½ *teaspoons poppy seeds*
1 *cup (41 percent) unsifted gluten flour* plus 2½ cups unsifted whole wheat flour*
cornmeal
egg glaze (1 egg yolk beaten with 1 teaspoon cold water)

*Gluten flour is available at health food stores.

152

If you used the onion in Stage One, fish it out of the sourdough mixture and discard. Dissolve the yeast in the warm water. Add the salt, caraway and poppy seeds, and yeast/water to last night's mixture. Stir. Add the gluten and whole wheat flour and stir to mix.

Knead the dough until smooth, either by hand on a floured board or with a dough hook. Put the kneaded dough in an ungreased bowl, cover, and let rise in a warm place until doubled in bulk—about 2 hours. Punch down and divide into 2 pieces.

Take each piece and form into a round loaf. Place the dough on a floured board, flatten it, and fold it into thirds, first from 1 direction and then the other. Pinch the dough to seal it and pat into a round shape.

Place the loaves on a greased baking sheet that has been sprinkled with cornmeal. Cover, and let rise in a warm place for about 30 minutes, until the dough is not quite doubled in bulk.

Just before baking, brush the tops of the loaves with the egg glaze. Bake the loaves in a preheated 425°F. oven for 40 to 50 minutes, or until the loaves are browned and sound hollow when tapped on the bottom. Do not hurry the baking: this rye bread takes a long time to cook thoroughly. If the loaves have a tendency to burn on the bottom, double up on the baking sheets. When the bread is cool enough to slice, butter a slice, rub the crust with garlic, and savor the taste of Heaven.

Yield: Makes 2 loaves, 20 slices each. *Each slice provides 82 calories.*

153

Dark Rye and Cornmeal Bread

Whole rye flour gives this bread a distinctive, earthy, satisfying flavor. The rye, which is low in gluten, gets a rising assist and some complementary nutrients from the whole wheat flour and the cornmeal. The trio makes a highly nutritious loaf that's practically a meal in every slice.

½ cup cornmeal
1 cup cold water
1 cup boiling water
1 tablespoon vegetable oil
2 teaspoons salt
2 tablespoons blackstrap molasses
2 teaspoons caraway seeds
1 tablespoon carob powder
2 tablespoons dry yeast
¼ cup warm water (110° to 115°F.)

2½ cups sifted dark rye flour (warmed to room temperature)
2 cups sifted whole wheat bread flour (warmed to room temperature)
½ cup wheat germ
cornmeal
egg wash (1 egg yolk beaten with 2 tablespoons water)
caraway seeds

Combine the cornmeal and the cold water. Add this mixture to the boiling water and stir until thickened. Stir in the oil, salt, molasses, caraway seeds, and carob powder. Dissolve the yeast in the warm water and add to the mixture. Stir well.

Blend in the flours and the wheat germ. Add a bit more warm water if necessary, but the dough should be a little sticky. Turn out onto a floured surface and knead well for 10 minutes, adding more flour if necessary.

Form the dough into a ball and place in a greased bowl, turning to coat the ball on all sides. Cover and place in a warm spot until it doubles in bulk—about 1 hour.

Punch the dough down and knead for a few minutes more. Form into 2 balls. Place on a greased cookie sheet sprinkled with cornmeal and allow to rise again until almost doubled in bulk—about 30 minutes. Brush with the egg wash, sprinkle with more caraway, and bake in a preheated 375°F. oven for 1 hour or until the loaf bottoms make a hollow sound when tapped.

Yield: Makes 2 loaves, 20 slices apiece. *Each slice provides 58 calories.*

Hearty Sunflower Pumpernickel

Unlike commercial pumpernickel, which is colored with a sugary caramel syrup and contains lifeless refined flours, this loaf is packed with health-promoting nutrients and many life-saving antioxidants. The sunflower seeds give it a delightful crunch.

*½ cup sunflower seeds, prefer-
    ably sprouted (when you
    sprout a seed, its nutrients
    skyrocket)*
2⅔ cups lukewarm water
2 teaspoons honey
4 teaspoons dry yeast
2 cups whole wheat bread flour

2½ cups whole rye flour
¼ cup soy flour
2 tablespoons wheat germ
2 tablespoons coarse bran
1 teaspoon salt (optional)
3 tablespoons blackstrap molasses
*3 tablespoons caraway, black
    caraway, poppy, or sesame
    seeds*

To sprout the sunflower seeds: The day prior to baking day, put ½ cup shelled sunflower seeds in 1 cup of lukewarm water. Use the soak water as part of the water allotment.

155

In a large bowl, combine 1 cup of the lukewarm water with the honey. Sprinkle the yeast over this mixture and place in a warm place to proof.

Warm the flours: Put the whole wheat in one bowl; in another bowl place the rye mixed with the soy, wheat germ, bran, and salt (if you're using it). Place in a warm oven (250°F) for about 15 minutes.

Add the warmed whole wheat flour to the activated yeast mixture and mix well. Add the molasses to ½ cup of the lukewarm water and add to the yeast mixture. Add the combined flour mixture and remaining water. Work in the sunflower seeds and your choice of caraway, sesame, poppy, or karnitchka (black caraway).

Spritz a large loaf pan (9 × 5 × 3 inches) with baking spray. Place the dough, which will be slightly sticky, in the prepared pan. (No need to knead this particular dough.) Sprinkle the top with more seeds of your choice. Place in a warm place to rise for about 1 hour. It will rise slightly but will not double in bulk.

Bake for 50 minutes, then test for doneness. Sometimes it requires a little more baking. When the bread is deliciously brown and crusty, remove it from the oven and cool on a rack for 10 minutes. Now turn it out of the pan onto the rack and allow it to cool completely before its appetizing aroma brings a stampede into the kitchen begging for a hunk.

Yield: Makes 1 two-pound loaf—30 slices. *Each slice provides 73 calories.*

Herbal Wheat Germ Challah

This is a flavorful in-between bread. If your family is still not ready for 100 percent whole wheat, this one will ease the transition. It's made with some white flour but with a lot of wheat germ to fill in the nutritional loopholes.

2 tablespoons dry yeast	1 cup water
1 cup unbleached white flour	¼ cup vegetable oil
½ cup soy flour	2 tablespoons honey
1 cup wheat germ	2 eggs
3 tablespoons coarse bran	1½ cups whole wheat bread flour
½ teaspoon salt (optional)	1 egg beaten with 1 teaspoon
½ teaspoon oregano	cold water for the egg wash
½ teaspoon marjoram	

In a large bowl, combine the dry yeast, white flour, soy flour, wheat germ, bran, salt (if you're using it), and herbs.

In a saucepan, combine the water, oil, and honey, and warm to about 120°F. Add this mixture to the yeast mixture.

Add the eggs and beat by hand or in a mixer for about 2 minutes. Now add the whole wheat flour. You should have a firm dough. Turn it out onto a floured board and knead for several minutes. Place the dough in a greased bowl and turn to grease all sides. Cover and let rise in a warm place until the dough has more than doubled in volume, or until the indentation remains when you push you finger into the dough.

Cut off 1/4 of the dough and divide it into 3 parts. Shape each part into a 10-inch strand. Braid the 3 strands together.

Divide the remaining dough into 3 portions, shape each portion into a 10-inch strand and braid them together in the same way. Place the large loaf in a 8 × 4 × 2-inch baking pan spritzed with baking spray. Place the little braid on top. Brush with the egg wash and sprinkle with your choice of seeds—sesame, poppy, or karnitchka (black caraway).

Cover and allow to rise again for about 45 minutes. Bake in a preheated 350°F oven for 30 minutes. Allow to cool slightly for a few minutes, then remove from the pan and cool on a wire rack. This bread enhances the flavor of all kinds of sandwiches. Try it with peanut butter, cheese, or tuna or chicken salad and enjoy!

Yield: Makes 1 beautiful loaf—20 slices. *Each slice provides 109 calories.*

Yogurt Bread with Wheat Germ and Bran

A high-rising high-protein loaf, rich in essential nutrients, with a refreshing flavor reminiscent of sourdough.

2 tablespoons dry baking yeast
¾ cup warm water
1¼ cups plain yogurt, warmed to
    room temperature
3½ cups whole wheat bread flour
½ cup soy flour
2 tablespoons unsalted butter,
    softened

2 tablespoons unsulphured
    molasses or honey
2 teaspoons baking powder
2 tablespoons wheat germ
2 tablespoons coarse bran
    yellow cornmeal
    melted butter
    sesame or sunflower seeds

In a bowl, add the yeast to the warm water and allow to stand for about 5 minutes or until the mixture bubbles.

In a separate bowl, combine the warmed yogurt, butter, and molasses or honey. In another bowl, combine 2½ cups of the whole wheat flour with the baking powder.

Add both mixtures to the yeast mixtures and beat, by hand or mixing machine, until all ingredients are well blended.

Combine the remaining whole wheat flour, soy flour, wheat germ, and bran. Add this mixture to the yeast mixture by hand and blend to make a stiff dough.

To make one large loaf, spritz a 9 × 5 × 3-inch loaf pan with non-stick baking spray. Cover the bottom with cornmeal.

For two loaves, divide the dough in half, prepare 2 pans about 8 x 4 inches, spritz with non-stick baking spray, and cover bottoms with cornmeal. Roll each half of the dough into a rectangle. Roll up tightly and tuck in the ends. Put the dough in prepared pans, brush with melted butter, and sprinkle with sesame seeds. Cover and let rise in a warm place until double in bulk—about 45 minutes.

Bake in a preheated 375°F oven for about 45 minutes until it's nicely browned. If it makes a hollow sound when you thump it, it's a well-baked bread.

Yield: Makes 1 large or 2 small loaves, a total of 30 slices. *Each slice provides 76 calories.*

Whole Wheat Pita

Pita is the pocket bread that is so convenient to fill with tuna, egg, or chicken salad, or whatever you're having for lunch. I like to cut pitas in halves horizontally, layer with melting cheese, tomato sauce, and a dash of garlic powder, oregano, and basil, and heat them in the toaster oven until the cheese melts. Kids call them instant pizza.

½ cup lukewarm water
1½ tablespoons dry baking yeast
1 teaspoon honey
2 cups lukewarm water
2 tablespoons olive oil
½ teaspoon herbal seasoner or
    crushed oregano

5 cups whole wheat bread
    flour
½ cup wheat germ
½ cup soy flour
1 egg white, beaten
    sesame or poppy seeds

Place the lukewarm water in a bowl and add the honey and yeast. Allow to proof for about 8 minutes.

In another bowl, combine the 2 cups of water with the oil and seasoner.

Combine the whole wheat flour with the wheat germ and soy flour. Make a well in the center of this combo and add the liquid mixture. Stir in the yeast mixture.

Knead the dough for about 5 minutes or until it begins to pull away from the sides of the bowl. Place in an oiled bowl. Brush the top with oil. Cover and set in a warm place to rise until double in bulk—about 50 minutes.

Punch the dough down. Roll the dough out on a floured surface to a thickness of about ¼ inch. Cut circles with a cookie cutter or the edge of a glass. Place one circle on top of another and press the outer edges together. Brush with the beaten egg white and top some with sesame seeds and others with poppy seeds. Let rise again for about an hour. Bake in a preheated 500°F oven, in the lower third of the oven, for 10 to 12 minutes or until golden brown.

Yield: Makes about 2 dozen pitas. *Each pita provides 104 calories.*

Tortillas

From south of the Border, these cornmeal pancakes have won fans all over the country. They're wonderful wrapped around a spicy bean filling. Even children who are non-eaters gobble them up.

1 cup whole wheat pastry flour
4 eggs, beaten
2 tablespoons peanut oil
1½ to 2 cups water

1 cup cornmeal, finely ground
½ teaspoon salt or vegetable seasoning

In a mixing bowl or food processor, blend together the eggs, oil, and 1½ cups water.

Combine flour, cornmeal, and salt or vegetable seasoning and blend this mixture with the egg mixture. Add a little more water if necessary to thin to the consistency of light cream. The amount of water needed will vary according to the coarseness of the cornmeal.

Dip a paper towel in a little oil, and wipe the bottom of a cast-iron skillet about 8 to 10 inches in diameter. On medium heat, preheat the skillet. Pour about ¼ cup batter into skillet and tilt or rotate pan, swirling the batter around easily to make a pancake about 6 inches across and ⅛ inch thick. Leave it a few minutes until it is brown on the bottom, then turn it over and leave it a short time to brown the flip side. Don't leave it too long or it may get too stiff to roll or fold.

To keep tortillas warm, stack them, cover with a tea towel, and put them in a warm oven.

Yield: Makes 24 tortillas.

Each tortilla provides 55 calories.

161

Wholesome Whole Wheat Challah

A high-protein, highly nutritious Sabbath twist. Two loaves of challah are placed on the Sabbath table to recall the double portion of manna that fell in the desert every Friday. Sliced challah makes wonderful toast to serve under poached eggs for breakfast.

2 tablespoons dry yeast or 2
    yeast cakes
½ cup lukewarm water
4 eggs
3 tablespoons olive or
    vegetable oil
1 tablespoon honey
1 teaspoon salt (optional)
2 cups hot water
4 cups whole wheat bread
    flour
½ cup soy, rice, or oat flour

3½ cups unbleached white or 3
    cups whole wheat
    pastry flour
1 cup unbleached white or
    popcorn flour
(To make popcorn flour, pop
    the corn, blenderize,
    then strain. Popcorn
    flour adds lightness to
    whole wheat flour.)
poppy, sesame, or caraway
    seeds to taste

Dissolve the yeast in ½ cup lukewarm water and set aside. Beat the eggs and reserve 2 tablespoons to be used for brushing the loaves later. In a large bowl, combine oil, honey, salt (if you're using it), eggs, and hot water. When the mixture cools to a bit hotter than lukewarm, add the yeast mixture. Mix well with a wooden spoon. Gradually add the 4 cups of whole wheat bread flour, reserving some for the kneading board. Mix well.

Combine remaining flours and add to the yeast mixture. Work them in. Let the dough rest for 10 minutes. Knead dough on a floured board for about 10 minutes. Add more flour if the dough is too sticky. Oil your hands for smoother handling.

Form the dough into a ball. Place the ball in an oiled bowl, and turn to grease all sides. Cover with a damp tea towel and set in a warm place (on a radiator or the back of the stove) for about 2 hours—until it doubles in bulk.

Punch the dough down and knead it again for a few minutes. Divide the dough in half and shape each half into a braided loaf.

To make a braid, divide each portion into 3 equal parts. Roll each part out a bit longer than the pan in which you plan to bake the challah. Pinch the strands together at one end. Then take the piece on the outer right, cross it over the middle one. Then take the piece on the outer left and also cross it over the middle. Repeat this procedure until you have completed shaping the bread. Pinch the strands together at the other end.

To make the challah extra fancy, divide the dough into 4 equal parts and make a thin braid out of the fourth section. Place this braid down the center of the large braid. This braid bakes up very crisp and is the nosher's crunchy delight.

After shaping the loaves, place both on a greased baking sheet, or in greased bread pans, and let them rise in a warm (not hot) place until double in bulk—for an hour or so.

Preheat oven to 400°F.

Add a teaspoon of water to the reserved egg and brush the surface of both loaves. Sprinkle with poppy, sesame, or caraway seeds.

When the loaves have risen, bake them for 15 minutes. Then reduce the heat to 350°F and continue baking for 45 minutes.

Yield: Makes 2 large loaves. Each loaf makes 20 slices.

Each slice provides 101 calories.

Note: Day-old challah makes marvelous French toast.

Challah dough is very versatile. Try shaping some of it into small round balls. Let them rise until double in bulk, brush with egg wash, top with sesame seeds, then bake on a greased baking sheet in a preheated 375°F oven for about 20 minutes. Use them as breakfast rolls, for tuna sandwiches, or hamburger buns. Make them long and narrow like hot dog rolls, then spread with peanut butter, fill with half a banana sliced lengthwise, and top with sunflower seeds. Even recalcitrant breakfast-snubbers love these.

Heavenly Brioche

These French rolls, first cousins to croissants, contribute a touch of class and a heavenly fragrance to any breakfast. Crunchy on the outside, light as a cloud on the inside, they're a breeze to make. They can be stored for as long as a week in the refrigerator or made part way and refrigerated overnight, or for several days. Then you can have fresh-from-the oven flavor and aroma to grace your breakfast or brunch table without any hassle.

3 to 4 cups unsifted whole wheat bread flour (not pastry flour)
½ teaspoon salt (optional)
1 package or 1 tablespoon active dry yeast
½ cup milk
¼ cup water

¼ cup honey
½ cup Healthy Heart Butter (see index for recipe)
3 eggs (at room temperature)
1 egg yolk
1 egg white, slightly beaten
2 tablespoons sunflower or sesame seeds

If you keep your flour in the freezer, as I do, warm it to room temperature, either by placing it in a conventional oven at 200°F for 10 to 15 minutes or by microwaving, uncovered, for 30 seconds on full power.

In a large mixing bowl, mix together 1 cup of the warmed flour, the salt, if you're using it, and the undissolved yeast.

In a saucepan, combine the milk, water, honey, and butter and heat over low heat until liquids are very warm (120° to 130°F). Butter does not have to melt. Add this mixture gradually to the dry ingredients and beat 2 minutes at medium speed, in electric mixer, scraping bowl occasionally. Add eggs, extra egg yolk, and ¾ cup of flour. Beat at high speed for 2 minutes, scraping bowl occasionally. Stir in enough additional flour to make a stiff batter.

Cover the bowl with plastic wrap or a tea towel, and let rise in a warm place until more than doubled in bulk—about 2 hours.

Stir the batter down and beat for 2 minutes. Cover tightly with plastic wrap and refrigerate for 2 hours or overnight.

Punch dough down and turn out onto a lightly floured board. Set aside about ¼ of the dough. Cut the larger piece into 24 equal pieces. Form each piece into a smooth ball and place in large well-greased muffin tins. Cut the small piece into 24 equal parts. Form into small balls.

With a moistened finger, make a deep indentation in center of each large ball. Press a small ball into each indentation. Cover and let rise in a warm place until doubled in bulk, in about 45 minutes.

Preheat oven to 350°F.

Bake for 25 minutes. Remove from oven and let cool in tins for 25 minutes. Remove from pans and place on wire rack to cool thoroughly. Wrap tightly in plastic bags and refrigerate up to 1 week.

To brown the brioche for your breakfast or brunch, place as many as you need in greased muffin tins. Brush them with slightly beaten egg white. Top with sunflower or sesame seeds and bake at 350°F for 12 minutes or until nicely browned. Remove from muffin tins and cool on wire rack, or serve hot. Any leftover browned brioche can be reheated in the toaster oven.

Yield: Makes 2 dozen.

Each brioche provides 117 calories.

Zucchini Date 'n' Nut Bread

Zucchini is a good source of vitamin A and potassium, and is incredibly low in calories.

½ cup chopped dates or raisins
2 cups grated unpeeled zucchini
3 eggs
⅓ cup olive or vegetable oil, or Healthy Heart Butter, softened (see index for recipe)
⅓ cup honey
1 tablespoon grated orange rind
1 teaspoon vanilla

2 cups whole wheat pastry flour
½ cup oat bran
½ cup rolled oats
3 tablespoons wheat germ
2 teaspoons baking powder
1 teaspoon baking soda
1 teaspoon cinnamon
½ cup chopped walnuts, pecans, or sunflower seeds

Preheat oven to 325°F.

Combine the dates and zucchini. Set aside.

In a large mixing bowl or food processor, blend together eggs, oil, honey, orange rind, and vanilla. Add the zucchini mixture.

In another bowl, mix together the flour, bran, oats, wheat germ, baking powder, baking soda, and cinnamon. Blend this mixture with the liquid ingredients. Stir in the chopped nuts.

Line 2 1-pound coffee cans, or any similar-sized cans with parchment paper or spritz them with nostick spray.

Divide the batter between the 2 cans and bake 1¼ hours.

Yield: Makes 2 loaves; each loaf makes 10 slices.

Each slice provides 152 calories.

Melt-in-Your-Mouth Quick Biscuits

There's nothing like a basket of crusty biscuits, hot from the oven, round and puffy, lightly browned on top, to fill you with that lovely feeling that Mom's in the kitchen, all's right with the world. Enriched with wheat germ and oat bran, these biscuits provide more than a nostalgic glow. They provide lots of nutrients for sustained energy and fiber for lowering cholesterol.

1½ cups whole wheat pastry
flour
2 tablespoons wheat germ
2 tablespoons oat bran
1 tablespoon baking powder

1 teaspoon vegetable seasoning
2 tablespoons poppy seeds
¼ cup reduced-calorie
mayonnaise
1 cup skim milk

Preheat oven to 450°F.

In a mixing bowl, sift the flour, wheat germ, oat bran, baking powder, and seasoning. Stir in the poppy seeds, mayonnaise, and milk. Mix to combine ingredients. Batter will be the consistency of thick cream.

Drop the batter by tablespoonfuls onto a large, ungreased cookie sheet.

Bake for 10 minutes or until the biscuits are golden.

Yield: Makes about 20 biscuits.

Each biscuit provides 52 calories.

Aunt Betty's Virginia Biscuits

Even the biscuits have a southern accent at Aunt Betty's. These are especially delicious when spread with unsweetened fruit conserves, but children often prefer them with peanut butter.

1½ cups whole wheat pastry flour	1 teaspoon vegetable seasoning
¼ cup oat bran	⅓ cup Healthy Heart Butter
2 tablespoons lecithin granules	(see index for recipe)
2 tablespoons wheat germ	2 teaspoons honey
1 tablespoon baking powder	⅔ cup buttermilk or yogurt

Preheat oven to 450°F.

In a mixing bowl, sift together the flour, oat bran, lecithin, baking powder, and seasoning. Remove ½ cup of this flour mixture and set aside.

Add the butter to the remaining flour mixture and blend it in with a pastry blender or 2 knives. Combine the honey and buttermilk, and stir until well blended. Add to the bowl.

Turn the dough out onto a lightly floured surface (use the reserved flour) and gently knead in all the remaining flour. Roll out the dough into a circle ½-inch thick. Using a 2-inch cutter or an inverted glass, cut out as many biscuits as possible. Place them 1 inch apart on a baking sheet, lightly greased or lined with parchment paper.

Bake in the middle of the oven 10 to 12 minutes or until the biscuits are golden brown.

Yield: Makes about 18 biscuits.

Each biscuit provides 71 calories.

Flaky Crescent Rolls

These tender, flaky rolls add a touch of elegance to breakfast and they are melt-in-your-mouth delicious.

2 tablespoons baking yeast
1 cup lukewarm water
1 cup vegetable oil or Healthy
    Heart Butter (see index
    for recipe)
3 tablespoons plus 1 teaspoon
    honey

1 cup warm water
3 eggs
6 cups whole wheat flour
1 teaspoon water
¼ cup sesame seeds

Dissolve the yeast in the lukewarm water. Stir in 1 teaspoon honey. Set aside for 5 minutes.

In a large bowl, mix the oil or butter, 3 tablespoons honey, and the warm water.

Beat 2 of the eggs. Add the beaten eggs and the yeast mixture to the oil mixture. Gradually stir in the flour, mixing well, but do not knead. Cover and chill in the refrigerator for about 2 hours.

Lightly oil a baking sheet or line it with parchment paper.

Turn the dough out onto a floured surface. Divide it into 3 parts and roll each part into a large circle as thin as possible.

Make an egg wash by combining the remaining egg with a teaspoon of water and brush evenly over rolled-out dough. Sprinkle with sesame seeds.

Cut each circle into wedges about 2 inches wide at the circumference. Roll each wedge toward the center. Dip the top in the egg wash and then in sesame seeds.

Place on prepared baking sheet and curve each roll slightly into the shape of a crescent. Let rise in warm place for 1½ hours.

Bake in preheated 400°F oven for 25 minutes or until golden. Serve warm. To reheat, wrap in foil and bake at 400°F for 5 minutes.

Yield: Makes 4 dozen rolls.

Each roll provides 98 calories.

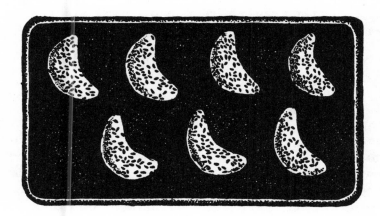

Old-Fashioned Cinnamon Buns

The very name of these fragrant, slightly sweet buns brings back memories of the tantalizing aromas in my Auntie Nina's kitchen and of her loving urging to "Eat, eat, you need your strength!" Believe me, nobody needed any urging to eat those warm, cinnamony "pultabulchas."

To make these delicious buns, you can use coffee-cake dough or challah dough. When you have challah dough, remove ⅓ of it after the first rising. Make a well in the center and add this mixture:

3 tablespoons softened butter	½ cup chopped pecans or
¼ cup honey	walnuts
1 teaspoon cinnamon	1 teaspoon grated orange peel
½ cup raisins or currants	

Combine these ingredients, then knead them into the dough.

Form into small rolls or flatten out egg-size portions, then fold 2 sides towards the center. Brush with egg wash (1 egg yolk beaten with 1 teaspoon cold water) and top with cinnamon and crushed nuts. Preheat oven to 350°F. Let rise again until they double in bulk. Bake for 25 to 35 minutes.

Yield: Makes approximately 12 pultabulchas.

Each pultabulcha provides 96 calories.

Whole Wheat Bagels

Bagels are now a very popular breakfast and snack food and have frequently been recommended as an energy-promoting complex carbohydrate. But, unless your bagel is made from whole wheat flour, it is not a complex carbohydrate—it is a simple carbohydrate food with not much to offer nutritionally.

Take a healthy tip and bake some bagels using high-energy whole wheat and soy flours with a little extra wheat germ and enjoy a satisfying nutritious treat.

1 cup of milk	3¼ cups whole wheat bread flour
¼ cup softened butter or vegetable oil	¼ cup soy flour
1 tablespoon honey or unsulfured molasses	¼ cup wheat germ
1 yeast cake or 1 tablespoon dry yeast	egg wash (1 egg yolk, beaten with 1 teaspoon cold water)
1 egg, separated	sesame, poppy, caraway, or chopped sunflower seeds

Combine the milk, butter or oil, and honey or molasses in a saucepan. Heat to lukewarm and add the yeast. Beat the egg white until frothy and add to the yeast mixture.

Combine the flours and wheat germ. Place half of the flour mixture in a large bowl. Make a well and add the yeast mixture. Stir until ingredients are well mixed. Add more flour if necessary to make a soft dough.

Sprinkle flour on the kneading board and work the dough on the board until it is smooth, then put the dough in a greased bowl and brush the top with oil or butter. Cover the bowl with a towel and place in a warm place to rise until double in bulk—about 1 hour.

Knead again on the floured board. Now break the dough into 4 pieces. Roll each piece into long strips about the width of your middle finger. Cut each strip into 6-inch pieces. Shape each piece into a circle and press the ends together. Let them relax on the board for about 10 minutes.

Now it's time for the water bath. Fill a large shallow pan with water and heat until very hot but not boiling. Drop the bagels in the hot water 2 at a time. When they rise to the surface, turn them over for another swim for just a few minutes.

To bake them, remove them from the water with a slotted spatula and place them on oiled cookie sheets. Mix the remaining egg yolk with the teaspoon of water and glaze each bagel using a pastry brush. Sprinkle the tops with your choice of sesame, poppy, caraway, and chopped sunflower seeds.

Bake in a preheated 425°F oven for 20 to 25 minutes until golden brown. Allow to cool on wire rack.

Yield: Makes about 16 bagels. *Each bagel provides 132 calories.*

Pumpernickel Bagels

These pumpernickel bagels get their dark color and whisper of sweetness from iron-rich blackstrap molasses.

2 tablespoons dry yeast
2 cups warm water or vegetable stock
1 tablespoon blackstrap molasses
3 cups whole wheat bread flour (warmed to room temperature)
1 whole egg plus 1 egg white

1 teaspoon low-sodium soy sauce
4 tablespoons olive or canola oil
2 cups whole rye flour, warmed
½ cup soy flour
4 quarts of water
1 egg yolk mixed with 1 teaspoon cold water for glaze
seeds for topping

Dissolve the yeast in ½ cup of warm water or stock mixed with ½ teaspoon of the molasses. Sift the whole wheat flour into a large bowl, then stir the yeast mixture into it. Add the whole egg, the egg white, the remaining warm water or stock, the rest of the molasses, the soy sauce, and the oil. Beat vigorously—by machine for 3 minutes, or by hand for 100 strokes.

Work in the combined rye and soy flours.

Turn the dough out onto a floured surface and knead for 10 minutes. Place the dough into an oiled bowl and turn to grease all sides. Cover the bowl with a towel and place in a warm place to rise. It should double its bulk in 1½ to 2 hours.

In a large pot, boil the 4 quarts of water.

Punch down the dough and knead briefly. Divide the dough into 18 round pieces the size of golf balls.

For miniature bagels, divide each ball in half.

To form the balls into bagels, poke your finger through the center of each. Let them rest for a few minutes before their bath.

THE BATH

Using a slotted spoon, place about 5 bagels at a time into the boiling water. Cook for 2 minutes on each side. Remove with the slotted spoon to an oiled cookie sheet. Repeat until all the bagels have had their bath.

Brush the bagels with the egg wash and sprinkle with poppy, sesame, or caraway seeds or with dehydrated chopped onion.

Bake in a preheated 325°F oven for about 30 minutes. Place on a wire rack to cool—if you can protect them from bagel-hungry kids.

Yield: Makes 18 average-size bagels or 36 miniatures. *Each average-size bagel provides 155 calories, and each miniature bagel provides 77 calories.*

MORE BAGELS

By following the same procedure as described in the recipe for Bagels, you can make these jolly circles in infinite variety.

Cinnamon Raisin Bagels

These are delicious both soft and toasted, and are a nutritious substitute for the high-fat Danishes, croissants, and tempting pastries that are frequently offered at the same time.

1 teaspoon cinnamon	1 teaspoon grated orange rind
1 teaspoon maple sugar	½ cup raisins

Mix together and knead into the dough after it has risen. For added crunch and nutritional value, top with chopped sunflower seeds.

Yield: Makes 20 average-size bagels or 40 miniatures. *Each average-size bagel provides 152 calories, and each miniature bagel provides 76 calories.*

Spelt Bagels

For those who are allergic to wheat, spelt bagels are a blessing. Spelt is an ancient grain mentioned in the Bible as one of the five grains indigenous to ancient Palestine.

Substitute spelt flour for the whole wheat or white flour and follow the same procedure as described in the recipe for whole wheat bagels.

Spelt provides the same calorie count as whole wheat.

Cinnamon Twist Coffee Cake
with Raisins and Nuts

So pretty, you can eat it with your eyes.

3 cups unsifted whole wheat
    bread flour (not pastry
    flour)
½ teaspoon salt (optional)
1 package or 1 tablespoon
    active dry yeast
½ cup milk
⅓ cup water

¼ cup honey
2 tablespoons butter
1 egg
½ cup raisins
1 teaspoon melted butter
½ cup chopped walnuts
2 to 3 tablespoons honey
1 teaspoon cinnamon

Warm the flour to room temperature by placing in conventional oven at 200°F for 15 minutes, or microwave, uncovered, for 30 seconds on full power.

In a large mixing bowl, thoroughly mix 1 cup of the flour, the salt, if you're using it, and the undissolved yeast.

In a saucepan, combine milk, water, honey, and 2 tablespoons of butter. Heat over low heat until liquids are very warm (120 to 130°F). Butter doesn't have to melt. Gradually add to dry ingredients and beat 2 minutes, at medium speed, in electric mixer, scraping bowl occasionally. Add eggs and ½ cup flour. Beat at high speed 2 minutes, scraping bowl occasionally. Stir in raisins. Add enough additional flour to make a stiff dough. Turn out onto lightly floured board; knead until smooth and elastic, about 8 to 10 minutes. Cover with plastic wrap, then a tea towel. Let rest 20 minutes.

Roll the dough into a 12-inch square. Brush lightly with melted butter. Combine walnuts, honey, and cinnamon. Spread one half of this mixture down the center third. Fold second third of dough over the center third. Spread with the remaining walnut mixture. Fold remaining third of dough over the 2 layers. Cut into strips about 1 inch wide. Take hold of each end of each strip and twist lightly in opposite directions (like wringing out a facecloth). Seal ends firmly. Arrange in a greased 9-inch-square pan. Cover loosely with buttered wax paper, then top with plastic wrap.

Refrigerate 2 to 24 hours.

When ready to bake, remove from refrigerator. Uncover dough carefully. Let stand at room temperature for 10 minutes.

Bake in oven preheated to 375°F about 30 minutes. Remove from pan and cool on wire rack.

Yield: Makes 1 scrumptious coffee cake (12 slices).

Each slice provides 200 calories.

MAKE YOUR OWN COOKIES

There's nothing like a cookie. A cookie cheers you when you're blue, keeps you company when you're lonely, keeps you from smoking. They're not very strong, but they can break the ice at a party. They go well with milk, tea, coffee, or lemonade, and they're nice to share with family, friends, and Fido.

There are times when we don't feel like eating a regular meal, or don't have the time to eat, or don't know what to eat. But who can refuse a cookie? Even a high-chair thumper who won't eat her Pablum will eat a cookie.

The problem with most cookies, though, is that they can make you fat, decay your teeth, give you a bellyache, and send you on a guilt trip. Smart Cookies are different—oh, so deliciously different. They're absolutely great for squelching the "I wants" and the "Gimmes," and marvelous for breaking the junk food habit because they have *no* empty calories.

Empty calories, such as those you get from refined sugar and bleached white flour, contain no body-nurturing nutrients—only fat-producing calories. Empty calories need vitamin B (especially B1, or thiamine) to be metabolized in your body. If you consume much sugar, and most of us do since it's hidden in so many of the commercial foods we buy, you're likely to suffer a deficiency in B1, which leads to fatigue, depression, and neuritis (pains in the joints).

Smart Cookies are dense in nutrients, each programmed to do a special job, without the abundance of fat and refined sweeteners found in ordinary cookies. They're rich in the vitamin B group to nourish your nerves and put a sparkle in your eyes; rich in calcium to strengthen your bones; rich in iron for your blood; rich in fiber to keep your colon healthy; rich in potassium for your heart; and chock-full of many other nutrients which I will tell you about with each recipe.

In addition, Smart Cookies are calorie-reduced. How do they compare with other cookies in the calorie department? Consider the following: oatmeal cookies made from a recipe in a popular cookbook provide about 125 calories each when they include chocolate chips; 110 calories without the chips (and most of these calories are empty). The comparable Smart Cookies, High-Flying Oatmeal Kites, contain just 50 hard-working calories each (none of them empty).

Honey spice cookies made from a recipe in a well-known women's magazine provide 180 calories each. A similar Smart Cookie, Mixed-Grain Peanut Almond Squares (made with honey and spices), provide only 70 calories.

Smart Cookies for babies, teens, and athletes have slightly higher calorie counts because of the increased energy requirements of these groups. But no cookies anywhere have more health-building nutrients.

Smart Cookies are for *everyone*. In addition to lunchbox and after-school goodies, and special ideas for your collegian's next survival package, you'll find wholesome morsels created for women "eating for two"; confections just right for your next dinner party or romantic tête-à-tête; snacks with magical energy-boosting ingredients perfect for marathon runners, aerobic dancers, parents chasing after small children, and executives struggling with the stress that comes with success; and much more. And although each chapter contains cookies that have been created to meet the needs of a different age group or activity, everyone will find tempting treats to enjoy on every page.

The cookies in this book accentuate the positive, eliminate the negatives, and multiply your chances of enjoying good health at every stage of life. And best of all, with these family-tested recipes, you'll find that in the pursuit of health and vigor, your taste buds never had it so good! As one nibbler put it at a lecture I gave recently, "All this, and heaven, too." Smart Cookies may pack a nutritional wallop, but their delectable flavors will make your tongue dance a jig.

Anyone who still doubts the taste excitement of wholesome food will swallow his skepticism with the first bite of a Smart Cookie. So turn the page, and get set to enjoy some smart snacking.

BAKING TIPS

The cookies in this book may be mixed by hand, blender, mixing machine, or food processor.

There are two basic types of cookies: those that are rolled out with a rolling pin, which should be thin and crisp; and those that are dropped from spoons, which are softer and contain more moisture than thin cookies.

If you should find yourself strapped for time to make individual drops, bake the dough in square or rectangular cake pans about 5 minutes longer than the directions call for, and then cut into squares. Thin cookie dough, also known as stiff dough, can also be shaped or cut out with special cookie cutters, as the occasion dictates—gingerbread people, Halloween witches, Thanksgiving pilgrims, Christmas Santas, Chanukah menorahs, and Valentine hearts. It can also be rolled, then sliced and baked, as for refrigerator cookies; shaped into balls; or pressed from a cookie press.

Most of the recipes in this book call for whole wheat pastry flour. Humidity and the size of the eggs (large eggs are recommended, but are not essential) affect the amount of flour needed. Too little flour means the cookies will spread; too much makes them tough.

To test for the right amount of flour, beat in almost all the flour required in the recipe. Touch the dough lightly with an unfloured finger. If your finger comes away sticky, add more flour—in small amounts to avoid excess.

To bake cookies, use cookie sheets rather than pans with sides, so the cookies can slide off. No sides also means better browning.

If you line your cookie sheets with parchment paper (found in gourmet cookware shops and some health-food stores), you will not need to grease or wash the pan. If you are not using parchment paper, try greasing the pan with a half teaspoon of liquid lecithin, combined with a half teaspoon oil.

Cookies will dry out if they bake too slowly, so place the oven rack on the top rung where browning is fastest, and be sure to preheat the oven.

Your cookies are finished when they are nicely browned. Wait a couple of minutes before you remove them with a wide spatula. Don't wait too long or they'll stick. If this should happen, return the pan to the oven for a minute.

Avoid storing crisp and soft cookies together. Crisp cookies will absorb moisture from the soft cookies and wilt. If crisp cookies have wilted, simply place them in a 300°F oven for 10 minutes.

Store a lemon, orange, or apple with soft cookies. The cookies will absorb the fruit's delicate flavor and remain soft.

Cookie dough wrapped in plastic wrap can be stored in the refrigerator for three months, or in the freezer for about six months. Baked cookies will keep about three weeks in the refrigerator and up to a year in the freezer.

SMART COOKIES FOR WOMEN
WHO ARE EATING FOR TWO

Whether you are pregnant or nursing a child, now is not the time to diet. Never in your life is what you eat so vital to the life of another. This is the time to enjoy good food. As Tom Brewer, M.D., writes in *Metabolic Toxemia of Late Pregnancy: A Disease of Malnutrition*, "Severe caloric restriction, which has been very commonly recommended, is potentially harmful to the developing fetus and to the mother. Mothers who gain an average of 36 pounds have babies with fewer abnormalites."

A few words of caution: at all other times, we advise throwing away the salt shaker. *But not during pregnancy.* You should salt to taste, and with good conscience. Sodium contributes to water retention, which is a good thing during pregnancy. Sodium helps maintain the increased blood volume needed to nourish the baby.

When you are nursing, there will be a heavy drain on your calcium supply. The baby has priority in this department even if the calcium he needs must be extracted from your bones. A good breakfast is important. Chances are you won't have time to prepare and eat an elaborate breakfast before the clarion call from the nursery. It's a good idea to have some of these cookies handy for nibbling. They are rich in protein, iron, calcium, and the whole vitamin B family, all of which helps to put the glow of health on you and your baby.

Along with a good diet, the cookies I have devised for you can help you enjoy nine months of glowing expectations—and give you the energy to enjoy the first months after your baby is born.

Crispy Ginger Satellites

Fly high with these delicious ginger cookies that really spice up your day. According to a recent study (*Lancet*, March 20, 1982), ginger may help subdue the collywobbles, motion sickness, and queasiness that many women experience in the early months of pregnancy. The milk powder, molasses, and wheat germ provide much-needed calcium and B vitamins. B1 (thaimine) and B6 (pyridoxine) have also been shown to relieve the nausea of pregnancy.

¼ cup butter
¼ cup molasses or honey
1 egg
½ teaspoon baking soda
¼ teaspoon salt
1 tablespoon water
2 cups whole wheat pastry
    flour, minus 2 tablespoons

2 tablespoons wheat germ
2 tablespoons milk powder
1 tablespoon ground ginger
    sunflower seeds for garnish
    (about ¼ cup)

In food processor, blender, or mixing bowl, blend butter, molasses or honey, and egg until smooth. Combine the baking soda, salt, and water and stir into the liquid mixture. Add the flour, wheat germ, milk powder, and ginger, and blend only until incorporated and dough is stiff.

Preheat oven to 350°F.

Pinch off pieces of dough the size of walnuts, flatten between your hands, and place on cookie sheet lined with parchment paper or greased with a mixture of a few drops of liquid lecithin and oil. Top

each cookie with sunflower seeds. For variety, leave some of the cookies unpressed, in the shape of walnuts. Bake for about 12 minutes. To maintain their delicious crispness, store in airtight container.
Yield: 3 dozen.
Approximately 50 calories each.

Happy Delivery Carob-Walnut Clusters

A crunchy, nutty celebration treat, rich in strengthening nutrients, and deliciously reminiscent of that old-time sweet shop flavor.

¼ cup butter	¼ teaspoon salt
¼ cup honey	½ cup whole wheat pastry
1 egg	flour
1½ teaspoons vanilla	1½ cups coarsely broken walnuts
5 tablespoons carob powder	

In food processor, blender, or mixing bowl, combine butter, honey, egg, and vanilla. Process or mix until smooth. Add the carob powder, salt, and flour. Mix until ingredients are well-combined, then stir in the walnuts.

Preheat oven to 325°F.

Drop the batter by teaspoonfuls onto a cookie sheet lined with parchment paper or greased with a mixture of a few drops of liquid lecithin and oil. Bake for 15 minutes.
Yield: 36 clusters.
Approximately 60 calories each.

Banana Pecan Tartlets

Bananas become incredibly sweet when they are frozen, making it unnecessary to add a concentrated sweetener. A delicious pick-me-up—something all mothers and mothers-to-be need!

1 cup mashed banana
⅓ cup sunflower seeds
3 tablespoons peanut butter
  (smooth or chunky)

1 teaspoon vanilla
½ teaspoon cinnamon
pecans and carob chips for
  garnish

In food processor, blender, or mixing bowl, combine banana, sunflower seeds, peanut butter, vanilla, and cinnamon, and blend until ingredients are well-mixed.

Line the cups of a muffin pan with paper liners. Place one heaping tablespoon of the batter in each. Top some with pecans and, for variety, some with carob chips. Place in freezer. Remove from freezer a few minutes before serving.

Yield: 12 miniature tarts.

Approximately 60 calories each.

High-Calcium Granola Pepita Squares

These unbaked, easy-to-make confections are a powerhouse of nutrients needed by mother and child. Calcium is necessary not only for bone and teeth formation, but also for blood clotting and for the nerves. Pumpkin seeds are rich in zinc, which recent research points to as necessary to the baby's future learning ability.

1 cup peanut butter (smooth or chunky)
½ cup dry milk powder
½ cup honey or molasses
½ cup wheat germ

1 cup granola (recipe follows)
½ cup coconut
2 tablespoons pepitas (pumpkin seeds), lightly toasted (or substitute sunflower seeds)

In food processor, blender, or mixing bowl, combine peanut butter and honey or molasses. Add dry milk, wheat germ, granola, and coconut, and mix well. Spread the mixture in a 9 × 13-inch dish lined with parchment paper or greased with a mixture of a few drops of liquid lecithin and oil, and press pumpkin or sunflower seeds into the mixture. Cut into 1½-inch squares and refrigerate or freeze.
Yield: 4 dozen.
Approximately 60 calories each.

CRUNCHY RAISIN GRANOLA

This power-packed granola mix is sweet and crunchy though it has no added fat or sweeteners. Eat it for breakfast and use it in all recipes calling for granola.

½ cup raisins	½ cup soy grits or flakes
1 cup hot water	¼ cup dry milk powder
3 cups uncooked rolled oats	1 teaspoon cinnamon
1 cup unsweetened shredded coconut	½ cup wheat germ
	¼ cup bran
½ cup sesame seeds	½ cup chopped or sliced
½ cup sunflower seeds	almonds (optional)

Soak the raisins in the water overnight or microwave on medium for 2 minutes.

Preheat oven to 250°F.

In a large bowl, combine the oats, coconut, sesame and sunflower seeds, soy grits or flakes, dry milk, cinnamon, and almonds (if desired). Mix in the wheat germ and bran.

Pour the water off the soaked raisins into a cup. Pour this raisin liquid over the oat mixture and mix to moisten the grains. Add the soaked raisins. Spread the mixture on two cookie sheets lined with parchment paper or greased with a mixture of a few drops of liquid lecithin and oil. Bake for one hour, stirring the mixture every 15 minutes. When the granola cools, store in tightly lidded containers. Keep refrigerated or frozen.

Yield: 2 quarts.

Approximately 400 calories per cup.

Peanut and Raisin Cookies

The combination of wheat, soy, and cornmeal, with their complementary amino acids, enriches these biscuit-like cookies with high-quality protein. The butters provide fat necessary to the development of baby's brain; wheat germ and raisins are good sources of iron; and the milk offers bone-building calcium. Keep some of these handy while you sit nursing the baby, and nibble in good health.

2 eggs
½ cup milk
¼ cup unsalted (sweet) butter
1 teaspoon grated nutmeg
1 teaspoon vanilla
⅔ cup peanut butter (smooth or chunky)
½ cup yellow cornmeal (preferably Hi-lysine)

1 cup whole wheat pastry flour, minus 2 tablespoons
2 tablespoons soy flour
1 teaspoon baking powder
¼ cup wheat germ
½ cup raisins
peanut halves or chunks for garnish

In food processor, blender, or mixing bowl, combine eggs, milk, butter, nutmeg, vanilla, and peanut butter. Blend until smooth.

In another bowl, combine the cornmeal, flours, baking powder, and wheat germ. Process or mix until ingredients are combined. Fold in raisins.

Preheat oven to 350°F.

Drop the batter by tablespoonfuls 2 inches apart on a cookie sheet lined with parchment paper or greased with a mixture of a few drops of liquid lecithin and oil. Garnish liberally with peanuts. Bake for 10 to 15 minutes or until deliciously browned.

Yield: 2 dozen.

Approximately 100 calories each.

Sesame Coconut Almond Cookies

Share these mouth-watering cookies with the love of your life. They are sky-high in potassium and rich in zinc, a trace mineral very important to growth, healing, and your sense of taste. And new research reveals that zinc is also important to the child's developing brain.

2 eggs
4 tablespoons butter
1/3 cup frozen orange juice
  concentrate, slightly thawed
2 tablespoons honey
1/2 teaspoon grated orange rind
1/2 teaspoon ginger
1 cup whole wheat pastry
  flour, minus 2 tablespoons
2 tablespoons soy flour
1 teaspoon baking powder

1/4 cup wheat germ
1/4 cup toasted almonds,
  chopped fine
2 tablespoons dry milk powder
1/2 cup unsweetened shredded
  coconut
1/2 cup dried currants or
  raisins (optional)
sesame seeds for garnish
  (approximately 1/4 cup)

In food processor, blender, or mixing bowl, combine eggs, butter, orange juice, honey, and rind, and blend until smooth and creamy.

Add the ginger, flours, baking powder, wheat germ, almonds, milk powder, and coconut. Blend just until ingredients are well-mixed. Fold in currants or raisins.

Preheat oven to 325°F.

Drop the batter by teaspoonfuls onto a baking sheet lined with parchment paper or greased with a mixture of a few drops of liquid lecithin and oil. Top each cookie with a liberal sprinkling of sesame seeds. Bake for about 25 minutes or until nicely browned.

Yield: 3 dozen.

Approximately 55 calories each.

Four-Grain Sunflower Cookies

These crisp, delicious cookies contain millet, one of the most well-balanced and least allergenic of all the grains, rich in protein, minerals, vitamins, and lecithin, which emulsifies cholesterol. Combined with the cornmeal, oats, and either wheat, rice, or amaranth flour, millet enhances the flavor and protein found in these very special cookies.

2 eggs
⅓ cup honey
¼ cup vegetable oil (preferably olive)
¾ cup buttermilk or yogurt
2 tablespoons frozen concentrated orange juice, slightly thawed
1 teaspoon vanilla

¼ cup millet
¼ cup cornmeal
¼ cup rolled oats, ground to a flour
1 cup whole wheat, rice, or amaranth flour
sunflower seeds for garnish (approximately ¼ cup)

In food processor, blender, or mixing bowl, combine eggs, honey, oil, buttermilk or yogurt, orange juice concentrate, and vanilla. Blend until smooth.

In another bowl, combine millet, cornmeal, oats, and flour. Add to egg mixture and process briefly till ingredients are combined.

Preheat oven to 300°F.

Drop dough from a tablespoon onto an ungreased cookie sheet. Top each cookie liberally with sunflower seeds. Bake for 30 minutes or until golden brown.

Yield: 3 dozen.

Approximately 40 calories each.

Chewy Apricot-Almond Granola Bars

Hippocrates must have been thinking of apricots and almonds when he said, "Let food be your medicine." A half cup of dried apricots provides 3½ milligrams of blood-building iron, some of the B vitamins, especially niacin, which is very important to maintain a pleasant dispositon, and a whopping 7,000 units of vitamin A, which helps you fight infection and which has recently been cited as an anti-cancer factor.

Almonds, too, are a nutritional miracle—an excellent source of protein (12 grams in a half cup), very rich in potassium, iron, calcium, and phosphorus, and high in essential polyunsaturated fatty acids, which tend to lower cholesterol levels. Apricots and almonds, plus the other wholesome ingredients in these confections, make them a wonderful afternoon pick-up.

While these are great for nursing mothers, the father of the baby can enjoy them too, as well as the baby's brothers and sisters. Take them along when you go shopping with your toddler—you'll be able to resist the junk food temptations during your trip.

1¼ cups rolled oats
½ cup sunflower seeds
1 egg, lightly beaten
2 tablespoons honey or
    molasses
½ cup peanut butter
    (smooth or chunky)
¼ cup wheat germ
2 tablespoons dry milk
    powder

½ teaspoon cinnamon
½ cup dried apricots,
    chopped
2 tablespoons raisins
    (optional)
½ cup almond slices, lightly
    toasted

Toast the oats and sunflower seeds on a cookie sheet in a 350°F oven for 5 to 7 minutes, or until dry and crisp.

In a saucepan over low heat, combine the lightly beaten egg, honey or molasses, and peanut butter. Stir with wooden spoon until ingredients are well-combined, then turn off heat.

Add the toasted oats and seeds, wheat germ, milk powder, cinnamon, apricots, and raisins.

Press the mixture into an 8-inch-square dish, lined with parchment paper or lightly oiled with a mixture of liquid lecithin and oil.

Press the toasted almonds over the top of the granola mixture. Cut into 1½-inch pieces and refrigerate or freeze.

Yield: 25 squares.

Approximately 65 calories each.

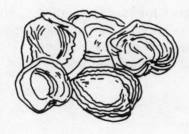

Carob Peanut Butter Bars

Crunchy sesame and sunflower seeds and creamy peanut butter merge with the chocolaty flavor of carob to form a sensational snack rich in vitamins and minerals, and very high in the potassium necessary to the smooth functioning of your heart, and your baby's.

¼ cup honey
2 tablespoons blackstrap
    molasses
1 teaspoon vanilla
½ cup peanut butter (smooth
    or chunky)
½ cup carob powder
½ cup sunflower seeds
½ cup sesame seeds

¼ cup wheat germ
½ teaspoon cinnamon
1 to 2 tablespoons water or
    orange juice (enough to
    achieve a smooth
    consistency)
unsweetened shredded
    coconut or chopped
    walnuts for garnish

In a medium-sized bowl, combine honey, molasses, vanilla, and peanut butter. Mix with wooden spoon until ingredients are combined.

Add the carob powder, seeds, wheat germ, and cinnamon, and mix. If mixture is dry, blend in the water or juice.

Spread the batter in an 8-inch-square ungreased dish. Press coconut or nuts over the surface. Cut into 1½-inch squares and refrigerate or freeze.

Yield: 25 squares.
Approximately 90 calories each.

SMART COOKIES FOR TEETHING BABIES, TODDLERS, AND PRESCHOOLERS

Children need to eat many of the foods their parents are cutting down on. So don't put the children on your diet!

You are very wisely limiting your calories and cutting down on fats, but bear in mind that babies and preschoolers need substantial amounts of fats and cholesterol to ensure the full development of their intellectual powers.

Eggs are one of the brain foods recommended by Ralph E. Minear, M.D., author of *The Brain Food Diet for Children.* Not only are eggs a good source of dietary fat, they are rich in lecithin, which, as I've mentioned, produces acetylcholine, one of the chemicals that acts as a transmitter for brain impulses within the body. Children need all kinds of fats, saturated, unsaturated, and cholesterol, Dr. Minear maintains. They are key elements in any diet that centers on brain development.

Children also need vitamins, minerals, and complex carbohydrates, all of which are provided in the Smart Cookies we have devised for your smart cookie.

Cookies to Cut Your Teeth On

Rich in calcium and iron, these cookies help to build strong teeth while they comfort sore gums. Your baby will chomp happily and in good health.

1 egg yolk, beaten
2 tablespoons blackstrap
   molasses
2 tablespoons vegetable oil
1 teaspoon vanilla extract

¾ cup whole wheat pastry
   flour
1 tablespoon soy flour
1 tablespoon wheat germ
1 tablespoon dry milk powder

In food processor, blender, or mixing bowl, blend the egg yolk, molasses, oil, and vanilla.

Preheat oven to 350°F.

Combine the flours, wheat germ, and milk powder, and add them to the egg mixture to make a dough. Roll the dough out on a lightly floured surface. Place the dough on a cookie sheet lined with parchment paper or greased lightly with a mixture of liquid lecithin and oil. Cut the dough into rectangles no bigger than a baby's finger.

Bake for 8 to 10 minutes. Cool on a wire rack.

Yield: 3 dozen.

Approximately 20 calories each.

Teddy Bear Treats

Give your toddlers a dish of grated carrots, raisins, seeds, and nuts and let them decorate their very own teddy bear cookies. If they eat some in the process, so who's counting?

½ cup vegetable oil
¼ cup honey
1 teaspoon vanilla
¼ cup orange or apple juice
½ teaspoon ginger
1 teaspoon cinnamon
2 cups whole wheat pastry flour

¼ cup soy flour
2 tablespoons wheat germ
raisins, currants, poppy seeds, apple butter, and nuts for decoration

In food processor, blender, or mixing bowl, combine oil, honey, vanilla, and juice. Blend until smooth and creamy.

Combine ginger, cinnamon, flours, and wheat germ, and add to the liquid mixture until it forms a dough. Divide dough into 4 pieces and wrap each in wax paper or plastic wrap. Refrigerate for an hour.

Preheat oven to 350°F.

Roll out each piece of the dough to a ¼-inch thickness. Cut each with a large round cookie cutter; you should be able to make two 3-inch circles out of each piece of dough, with some left over, which we will soon put to work.

Place four of the circles at the top of a cookie sheet lined with parchment paper or greased with a mixture of a few drops of liquid lecithin and oil. Using a finger, make two indentations in each of the circles to form wide eyes. Place a dab of the apple butter in each. Add little bits of the leftover dough to the sides of the four circles to form ears. (Moisten the joints with a little water to more effectively attach the body parts.)

Attach the remaining four circles underneath the heads to form pudgy bodies. If you are feeling creative, make fat arms and legs with leftover dough. Use raisins, currants, poppy seeds, or nuts for additional trimming.

Bake for 10 to 15 minutes. Let them cool for a minute, then remove to a wire rack.

Yield: 4 large bears.

Approximately 500 calories in each bear—about 10 calories a nibble.

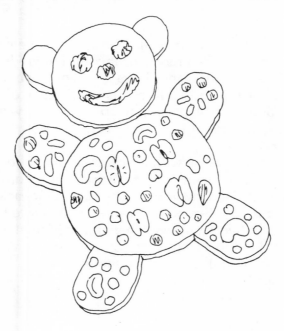

Molasses Peanut Butter Alphabet Letters

The children will be eating their words and loving every bite of these delicious morsels, which provide wholesome nutrients while introducing them to the alphabet in a most delightful way.

1 egg
⅓ cup blackstrap molasses
½ cup peanut butter (smooth or chunky)
1 teaspoon vanilla

⅓ cup carob powder
1 cup whole wheat pastry flour, minus 2 tablespoons
2 tablespoons soy flour
sesame seeds (about ¼ cup)

In food processor, blender, or mixing bowl, combine egg, molasses, peanut butter, and vanilla. Process or mix until ingredients are well-blended. Combine the carob and flours in a separate bowl and add to the egg mixture. The mixture will be the consistency of dough.

Divide the dough in 4 pieces, wrap in plastic wrap or waxed paper, and refrigerate for at least one hour.

Preheat oven to 325°F.

Grease two cookie sheets with a mixture of liquid lecithin and oil, or line them with parchment paper. Remove one portion of dough from the refrigerator and cut it into 12 pieces. Roll each piece into a 6-inch rope, and roll each rope in sesame seeds. Place them one at a time on the cookie sheets and twist them into different letters. Repeat with the rest of the dough, but save some dough to make the letters of your child's name. Bake for 8 to 10 minutes.

Yield: 4 dozen letters.

Approximately 35 calories each.

Rice Pudding Cookies

As dessert or as a special treat, these cookies fit the bill. Take some along on a shopping trip and share them with your toddler. They're rich in those great B vitamins that put a nice glow on your disposition—and on baby's.

1 egg
¼ cup butter, softened
*¼ cup frozen apple or orange
    juice concentrate, slightly
    thawed*
*2 tablespoons molasses, maple
    syrup, or barley malt syrup*
2 teaspoons vanilla
1 cup cooked brown rice
*1 cup whole wheat pastry
    flour, minus 2 tablespoons*

2 tablespoons soy flour
1 teaspoon baking soda
3 tablespoons wheat germ
1 teaspoon cinnamon
*¼ teaspoon freshly grated or
    powdered nutmeg*
*½ cup currants or raisins
    carob chips and coconut for
    garnish*

In food processor, blender, or mixing bowl, combine egg, butter, fruit juice, sweetener, vanilla, and rice. Mix until well-blended.

In another bowl, combine the flours, baking soda, wheat germ, cinnamon, and nutmeg. Mix briefly to combine ingredients. Fold in the currants or raisins.

Preheat oven to 350°F.

Drop the batter by teaspoonfuls onto a cookie sheet lined with parchment paper or greased with a mixture of liquid lecithin and oil. Press down with a wet fork. The thinner the dough, the crisper the cookies will be. Garnish each with a few carob chips and some coconut. Bake in upper third of oven for 12 to 15 minutes.

Yield: 4 dozen.

Approximately 50 calories each.

Butterfly Ginger Cookies

Let the kids draw pretty shapes onto the wings of these butterfly-shaped cookies with a delicious cream cheese icing flavored with orange.

⅓ cup vegetable oil
½ cup blackstrap molasses
3 cups whole wheat pastry
    flour
¼ cup soy flour
1 teaspoon baking soda

½ teaspoon cinnamon
½ teaspoon ginger
⅓ teaspoon cloves
¼ cup orange juice or water
    currants

CREAM CHEESE ICING

4 ounces of cream cheese
2 tablespoons frozen orange
    juice concentrate,
    slightly thawed

In food processor, blender, or mixing bowl, combine oil and molasses and blend until light and smooth. In another bowl, combine flours, baking soda, cinnamon, ginger, and cloves, and add to the molasses mixture. Blend. Add orange juice or water as needed to make a pliable dough. Chill about one hour.

Preheat oven to 350°F.

Draw a butterfly outline about 4 inches long onto cardboard with your child's assistance. Cut it out and grease one side of it. Roll half the dough at a time to ¼-inch thickness. Lay the butterfly pattern

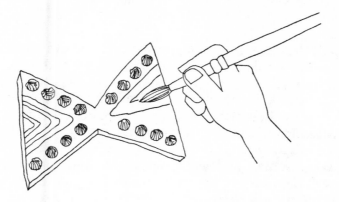

greased side down on the dough and cut around it with a sharp knife. Using a broad spatula, lift the dough onto a baking sheet lightly greased with a mixture of liquid lecithin and oil. Repeat procedure, or for variety, cut out other patterns. Store-bought cookie cutters can also be used.

Bake in the upper third of the oven for 12 minutes or until cookies spring back when gently tapped in the middle. Take them from oven before they brown and let them cool a few minutes before removing them to a wire rack.

Blend the cream cheese and orange juice concentrate until smooth. When the cookies are cold, decorate the butterflies using currants and the cream cheese frosting, which can be applied with a slim paint brush.

Yield: 20 butterflies.
Approximately 115 calories each.

SMART COOKIES THAT GO TO SCHOOL
IN POCKET OR LUNCHBOX

These top-of-the-class nutty nuggets work two ways to help your child make the grade at school and cope with the difficult pre-adolescent years. First, they eliminate the negatives—the over-sweetened, oversalted, over-processed foods that lead to cavity corners, climb-the-wall hyperactivity, and muddle-headed mentality. Second, these cookies are rich in the nutrients necessary for health, vitality, and creative thinking skills.

These wholesome cookies may not make your child a genius, but they sure will help him or her fulfill his or her greatest potential.

To facilitate the preparation of these special confections, I suggest you keep on hand a supply of my special Dynamite Mix, a basic dough that is used for many of the recipes in this book (you'll see it in the lists of ingredients).

DYNAMITE MIX

1 cup sunflower seed meal
(grind sunflower seeds
in a seed mill or coffee
grinder)
1 cup wheat germ
1 cup oat flour (process rolled
oats in a blender)

1 cup corn meal (preferably
Hi-lysine)
1 cup soy flour
½ cup dry milk powder
½ cup brewer's yeast
1 cup rice flour

Combine ingredients and store in the freezer, in a jar or plastic bag. Since many recipes in this book call for one cup of this mix, it would facilitate preparation if you stored one cup to one bag.

Any one of these ingredients may be omitted if you don't have it on hand or have an allergy to it. There are approximately 420 calories in one cup of Dynamite Mix.

School-Days Breakfast Bars

A good breakfast will keep your child's blood sugar levels on an even keel so they don't lag in the middle of the morning. These scrumptuous chewy granola bars can be eaten with your breakfast or, when you are rushed, instead of breakfast. They're rich in protein, complex carbohydrates, vitamins, and minerals. And take some along for lunch to prevent mid-afternoon slump.

1 egg
1 teaspoon vanilla
½ cup peanut butter
⅓ cup molasses or honey
2½ cups toasted oats (toast on cookie sheet for 15 minutes in 350°F oven)

1 cup Dynamite Mix (page 206)
1 teaspoon cinnamon or grated orange peel
1 cup raisins
1 cup chopped nuts

In food processor, blender, or mixing bowl, combine egg, vanilla, peanut butter, and molasses or honey, and process till well-mixed. In another bowl, combine the oats, Dynamite Mix, and cinnamon or orange peel, and process until ingredients are mixed. Add raisins and nuts.

Preheat oven to 350°F.

Press the mixture firmly into a 10 × 15-inch jelly-roll pan, well greased with a mixture of liquid lecithin and oil, or lined with parchment paper. Bake for 20 minutes. Cool slightly, then cut into 2-inch bars. Store in a tightly covered container in the freezer.
Yield: 40 bars.

Approximately 85 calories each.

Outer Space Saucers

They're out of this world—and chock-full of get-up-and-go nutrients. I can't make enough of them when my grandchildren are around. They're also great to make along with your children, because there is no baking involved. You can eat these right from the freezer or take them along. This cookie is a candy you can feel good about.

1 cup peanut butter (smooth or chunky)
⅓ cup honey
¼ cup carob powder
1 cup raisins
1½ cups granola (page 190)

In a medium-sized bowl, combine peanut butter and honey, mixing with a wooden spoon. Mix in the carob powder, then fold in the raisins and granola. It will make a fairly stiff dough. Take handfuls of the dough and roll each on waxed paper into the shape of fat cigars. Place the cigars in the freezer.

When they are hard but not yet frozen solid, slice the cigars into nickel-sized pieces. If the cigars should get frozen, simply leave them at room temperature for a few minutes until they are thawed enough to slice.

Yield: about 8 cigars and a zillion "saucers."
Approximately 350 calories in each cigar.

Big Banana Bozos

These nutty crunchies are fortified with brewer's yeast for extra protein to rev up your motor, and blackstrap molasses for blood-enriching iron.

⅔ cup whole wheat pastry
  flour
2 tablespoons soy flour
2 tablespoons wheat germ
2 tablespoons brewer's yeast
⅓ cup dry milk powder
1 teaspoon cinnamon
½ teaspoon powdered ginger
½ teaspoon nutmeg
½ cup chopped cashews,
  lightly roasted
½ cup sunflower seeds, lightly
  roasted

¼ cup vegetable oil
3 tablespoons blackstrap
  molasses
2 tablespoons honey
1 egg
1 large banana, mashed
  (about 1 cup)
½ cup raisins, or unsweetened
  carob chips, or some of
  each
peanuts or carob chips for
  garnish

In a bowl, mix together the flours, wheat germ, yeast, milk powder, cinnamon, ginger, and nutmeg. Set aside.

In food processor, blender, or mixing bowl, combine oil, molasses, honey, egg, and mashed banana, and mix until light and fluffy. Add the dry ingredients and process until combined. Stir in the nuts, seeds, and carob chips or raisins.

Preheat oven to 325°F.

Drop the batter by tablespoonfuls onto two cookie sheets lined with parchment paper or greased with a few drops of liquid lecithin and oil. Top each cookie with several peanut halves or carob chips. Bake for 12 to 15 minutes or until firm. Transfer cookies to wire rack to cool.

Yield: 3 dozen.
Approximately 80 calories each.

Butter Pecan Touchdowns

Take some to the game and you'll be sure to score!

¼ cup unsalted (sweet) butter,
   cut in slices
¼ cup honey

or 1¼ cups
Dynamite
Mix
(page 206)
{ 1 cup whole wheat pastry
   flour
2 tablespoons wheat germ
2 tablespoons dry milk powder

½ cup chopped pecans
1 cup chopped dates or figs,
   or a mixture of the two
½ cup orange or apple juice
½ cup unsweetened shredded
   coconut, lightly toasted

Cook the dried fruit in the fruit juice until thick (about 15 minutes), microwave on medium for 2 minutes, or, if you have time, simply soak the fruit in the juice overnight.

Preheat oven to 375°F.

In food processor using the steel blade, or in blender or mixing bowl, cream together the butter and honey. Add flour, wheat germ, and dry milk, and process only until these are incorporated into the mixture. Stir in the pecans.

Spread the mixture in an ungreased pie plate as thin as possible, using a spatula. Bake for 15 minutes, then break it up into large crumbs and bake for 5 minutes longer until golden brown and crisp.

Let cool, then combine with the toasted coconut. Puree or mash the dried fruit mixture and combine it with the crunchy mixture. Roll the mixture into a cylinder about 2 inches in diameter. Roll in chopped pecans. Press the roll into an oval shape and refrigerate for several hours or overnight. Slice into ¼-inch football-shaped cookies.
Yield: about 2½ dozen.
Approximately 75 calories each.

High-Flying Oatmeal Kites

Full of crunchy goodies that make you feel you're on top of the world.

¼ cup unsalted (sweet) butter,
    cut in slices
¼ cup honey
⅓ cup peanut butter, smooth
    or chunky, or tahini
    (sesame butter)
1 teaspoon vanilla
1 egg

½ cup whole wheat pastry
    flour
¼ cup wheat germ
¼ cup rolled oats
2 tablespoons soy flour or soy
    grits
2 tablespoons dry milk powder
½ teaspoon baking soda
½ cup raisins

} or 1¼ cups Dynamite Mix (page 206)

Combine the butter, honey, peanut butter or tahini, vanilla, and egg in food processor, blender, or mixing bowl, and mix until smooth and creamy.

Combine the flour, wheat germ, oats, soy flour, milk powder, and baking soda and add to the wet ingredients. Blend briefly, then mix in the raisins.

Preheat oven to 325°F.

Line a cookie sheet with parchment paper or grease it with a mixture of a few drops of liquid lecithin and oil.

The cookie batter will be thick. Take pieces about the size of a walnut and press onto the cookie sheet in a diamond shape, like a kite. Bake 8 to 10 minutes or until pale gold. Remove to wire rack to cool, and store in an air-tight container so that they will retain their delicious crunchiness.

Yield: 3 dozen.

Approximately 50 calories each.

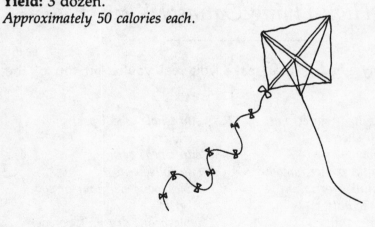

Smart-Aleck Snaps

Full of good B vitamins that help you keep your cool, these lemon-flavored cornmeal pecan cookies perk up the lunchbox and are a delicious after-school snack. Make a big batch—they freeze well. Your kids will enjoy a few before the big game or exams.

1 cup whole wheat pastry
    flour
or 1¼ cups (2 tablespoons soy flour
Dynamite) 2 tablespoons wheat germ
Mix } 2 tablespoons bran
(page 206) (2 tablespoons powdered milk
½ cup cornmeal (preferably
    Hi-lysine)
1 teaspoon baking powder
½ teaspoon baking soda
¼ cup butter or vegetable oil
½ cup honey or maple syrup

1 egg
2 teaspoons finely grated
    lemon zest (lemon peel)
2 tablespoons lemon juice or
    orange juice
½ cup buttermilk, sour milk,
    or yogurt
½ cup finely chopped pecans,
    walnuts, or peanuts
chopped pecans, almonds,
    or carob chips for
    garnish (about ½ cup)

Preheat oven to 325°F.

Stir together all the dry ingredients in a bowl. In food processor, blender, or mixing bowl, beat the butter and honey together, then add the egg, lemon zest, juice, and buttermilk and process until smooth and creamy. Add the dry ingredients and mix briefly until incorporated. (If you are using an electric mixer rather than a food processor, follow the same procedure, except that you would add the buttermilk alternately with the mixture of dry ingredients.) Stir in the chopped nuts.

213

Drop the batter by teaspoonfuls onto an ungreased cookie sheet 2 inches apart, to allow for spreading. Garnish with nuts or carob chips. Bake for about 12 minutes. Watch the cookies carefully, as they burn easily. Remove to a wire rack to cool.

Yield: 4 dozen.
Approximately 50 calories each.

Good Scout Coconut Gems

If there are boy or girl scouts meeting at your house, they'll do their darndest to deserve these dreamy confections that will delight their tastebuds while providing the nutrients they thrive on. Use cottage cheese for more protein; cream cheese for a smoother texture—or combine the two for a velvety batter with a nutritional wallop.

BOTTOM LAYER:
- ¼ cup unsalted (sweet) butter, softened
- ¼ cup cottage cheese (drained), or cream cheese
- 1 teaspoon vanilla
- ¼ cup honey
- 1¼ cups whole wheat pastry flour or Dynamite Mix (page 206)

TOP LAYER:

¼ cup yogurt
3 tablespoons molasses
2 tablespoons honey
2 tablespoons dry milk powder
3 tablespoons whole wheat
   pastry flour
½ teaspoon baking soda

½ cup chopped nuts (pecans,
   walnuts, or peanuts)
½ cup sunflower seeds
1 cup unsweetened coconut
   shreds
carob chips for garnish

Preheat the oven to 325°F.

Combine the butter, cheese, vanilla, ¼ cup honey, and 1¼ cups flour in a food processor, blender, or mixing bowl. The mixture will have a dough-like consistency. Spread the batter into an 8 × 12-inch baking dish lined with parchment paper or greased with a few drops of liquid lecithin and oil. Bake for about 20 minutes.

In a medium-sized bowl, combine the yogurt, molasses, 2 tablespoons honey, milk powder, 3 tablespoons flour, baking soda, nuts, and seeds. Process or mix to combine ingredients.

Pour this mixture over the baked bottom layer (it does not have to be cooled). Top the mixture with coconut. A very nice touch would be to inscribe with carob chips the name of a boy or girl scout whose birthday is imminent. If no birthday is pending, inscribe a message such as "Scouts are tops." Bake another 10 to 15 minutes. Cut into 1½-inch squares. They'll love it!

Yield: 28 squares.

Approximately 100 calories each with the cream cheese; 85 calories each with the cottage cheese.

SMART COOKIES FOR
THE NONSTOP TEENAGER

At the time in their lives when they need the very best nutrition, they are getting the worst. Here's how to help them.

Even though your teenager seems to be forever eating, studies indicate that teenagers are actually the poorest-fed members of the American family. They tend to skip breakfast because they are rushed. Some will skip lunch, too, in a misguided search for a slinky figure. They tend to subsist on snacks, candy bars, and soft drinks—empty-calorie foods made chiefly of fat and sugar, woefully lacking in the vitamins, minerals, protein, and carbohydrates their growing bodies so desperately need.

What happens? Contrary to their public image, teenagers are not full of boundless vim, vigor, and exuberant good health. Many of them suffer from fatigue, anemia, scoliosis, acne, anorexia, and depression.

Help them to understand the importance of providing the right fuel for their growing bodies. Encourage good, wholesome breakfasts and sit-down meals with the family in a congenial, loving ambience, and, since they are inveterate snackers, provide them with snacks that will give their growing bodies the essential nutrients. The rewards in radiant health, upbeat attitude, and personal achievement cannot be calculated.

Battery-Charging Apricot Chews

These tasty gems, easy to stash in your purse or pocket, provide many of the nutrients often lacking in the teenage diet. Apricots and molasses provide a big dollop of iron (about 1.3 milligrams in each slice), which is especially low in the diets of teenage girls, as well as vitamin A, so important to the body's immune reaction, and calcium for growing bodies. Since these delicious confections require no baking, kids can enjoy making a quick batch for pajama party snacking.

12 dried apricots
  apple or orange juice (for
    soaking the apricots)
 6 dried figs
½ cup raisins
½ cup almonds

½ cup sunflower seeds
 2 tablespoons blackstrap
    molasses
½ cup wheat germ
  coconut flakes

Soak apricots and figs in apple or orange juice for a few hours or overnight or microwave on medium for 2 minutes. Drain. Retain juice for another purpose, or drink it.

Combine the apricots, figs, raisins, almonds, seeds, molasses, and wheat germ in food processor or blender. Process until ingredients are finely chopped.

On wax paper, form the batter into a sausage-like roll. Cover with coconut. Refrigerate for a few hours, then slice or form into balls.
Yield: 2 dozen ½-inch slices or walnut-sized balls.
Approximately 76 calories each.

Pumpkin-Seed Cookies

These cookies are chock-full of pumpkin, which is rich in vitamin A, and pumpkin seeds, which provide a bounty of zinc and calcium—nutrients essential to a lovely complexion.

1 egg
1 cup mashed pumpkin
  (canned or homemade)
¼ cup unsalted (sweet) butter
  or oil (olive or
  vegetable)
2 teaspoons vanilla
¼ cup honey
2 tablespoons molasses
1 cup whole wheat pastry
  flour

¼ cup wheat germ
2 tablespoons dry milk powder
½ teaspoon baking soda
1 teaspoon cinnamon
¼ teaspoon nutmeg
¼ teaspoon ground cloves
1½ cups rolled oats
½ cup raisins
1 cup pumpkin seeds, coarsely
  chopped

Preheat oven to 350°F.

In food processor, blender, or mixing bowl, combine the egg, pumpkin, butter or oil, vanilla, honey, and molasses. Process until smooth and creamy.

In a medium-sized bowl, combine the flour, wheat germ, milk powder, baking soda, cinnamon, nutmeg, cloves, and oats. Add to the pumpkin mixture and process briefly. Fold in the raisins and pumpkin seeds. Drop the batter by teaspoonfuls on cookie sheets lined with parchment paper or greased with a mixture of a few drops of liquid lecithin and oil. Bake for 15 minutes or until firm and golden brown. Cool on wire rack.

Yield: 4 dozen.

Approximately 45 calories each.

Pure Pleasure Maple Banana Cheesecake Tarts

A real low-calorie treat for the palate, with a bonanza of wholesome nutrients for body and soul. Soaking the sunflower seeds starts the sprouting process, which causes the nutrients to skyrocket. My ballerina granddaughter loves these, she says, "because they taste like a zillion calories but they don't make you fat!"

CRUST

½ cup sunflower seeds, soaked overnight in water

½ cup graham cracker crumbs, or your own cookie crumbs

FILLING

1 egg
1 banana
3 ounces ricotta cheese (drained) or cream cheese
1 teaspoon vanilla

1 tablespoon maple syrup granules
blueberry or strawberry preserves, unsweetened (Sorrell Ridge is a good brand)

In food processor, blender, or mixing bowl, combine sunflower seeds and crumbs. Place a teaspoon of this mixture in 12 cups of a miniature muffin pan, lined with paper liners. (You can also use regular size muffin tins.)

Preheat oven to 350°F.

Combine the egg, banana, cheese, vanilla, and maple syrup granules in mixer, blender, or food processor, and mix until smooth and creamy. Place one tablespoon of the cheese filling in each tart shell.

Bake for 20 minutes. Top each tart with a half teaspoon of fruit preserves. Store in refrigerator or freezer. Defrost a few minutes before serving.

Yield: 12 miniature tarts or 6 muffin-sized ones.

Approximately 88 calories each with cream cheese; 72 calories each with ricotta (larger tarts contain twice the calories).

Fruit and Nut Bars

Soaking the almonds starts the sprouting process, causing an explosion of nutrient values and the development of vitamin C, which helps the body utilize the calcium-rich ingredients so necessary for strong healthy bones. The pineapple, dates, and coconut provide a medley of flavors to delight your taste buds.

2 eggs
½ cup drained crushed
    pineapple (reserve juice)
½ cup almonds soaked in
    reserved pineapple juice
    (for 2 hours or overnight)
¼ cup molasses or
    honey

½ cup chopped dates
½ cup shredded coconut,
    unsweetened
½ cup whole wheat pastry
    flour
¼ cup dry milk powder
¼ cup wheat germ

Drain the crushed pineapple, reserving the juice, and soak the almonds in the juice for two hours or overnight.

Preheat oven to 350°F.

In food processor, blender, or mixing bowl, combine eggs, pine-apple, almonds, molasses, dates, and coconut, and mix until well-combined. Add the flour, milk powder, and wheat germ, and mix briefly.

Spread the mixture in a 9-inch-square baking dish lined with parchment paper or greased with a few drops of liquid lecithin and oil. Bake for 30 minutes or until golden and firm. Cool slightly, then cut into 1½-inch squares.

Yield: 36 squares.

Approximately 45 calories each.

Energy-Packed Date and Sesame Brownies

Chewy date-and-nut filling between the crunchy layers of these brownies make them an ambrosial treat, bound to boost your morale and your energy quotient.

2 eggs
¼ cup honey
¼ cup butter
¼ cup milk
¼ cup carob powder
¼ cup whole wheat flour
¼ cup wheat germ
2 tablespoons dry milk powder

1 teaspoon baking powder
¾ cup sesame seeds
1 cup pitted dates, finely chopped
½ cup raisins
½ cup chopped nuts or sunflower seeds

Preheat oven to 325°F.

In food processor, blender, or mixing bowl, combine eggs, honey, butter, and milk. Blend until smooth and creamy.

In a mixing bowl, combine carob powder, flour, wheat germ, milk powder, baking powder and sesame seeds. Add to the egg mixture and process just until ingredients are well-blended.

In another bowl, combine the dates, raisins, and nuts. Pour half the batter into a baking pan about 8 × 13 inches, lined with parchment paper or greased with a mixture of liquid lecithin and oil.

Spread the mixture of dates, raisins, and nuts over the bottom layer, then cover with the rest of the batter. Bake for 30 minutes. Allow to cool slightly, then cut into 2-inch squares.

Yield: 32 squares.

Approximately 90 calories each.

SMART COOKIES THAT GO
TO COLLEGE/SURVIVAL SNACKS

The food in most college dining rooms is usually highly salted, highly sugared, over-processed, and lacking in the nutrients essential to health and vitality. I receive letters about it from students all over the country. "The food here is awful," they say. "I find myself filling up on starches, my skin is breaking out, I'm always tired, and I have trouble keeping up with my work."

The college years can be a real drain on the body's resources, and when the body lacks even one essential nutrient, the mind may suffer a slow-down.

When our kids were at college, I used to send what they call "Mom's Care Packages"—dried fruit, homemade granola, vitamin C tablets, and cookies, cookies, cookies.

As a footnote, I must mention that our kids missed very few days due to illness; all four made the dean's list and three of them qualified for Phi Beta Kappa.

To mail cookies, stack them tightly in a tin box with a tight-fitting lid or in a sturdy cardboard box. Use plenty of filler material in the bottom of the container, on top of the cookies, and in all the empty spaces. Filler can be crushed waxed paper or foil, but the filler our kids liked best was popcorn. It's lightweight, it provides good insulation against breakage, and it's edible.

Maple Walnut Nuggets

The lovely flavor of maple and the delicious crunch of walnuts make these little gems a welcome and wholesome companion for-late night cramming.

3 tablespoons butter
1 egg
¼ cup maple syrup granules
½ teaspoon vanilla
¾ cup rolled oats
½ cup whole wheat pastry
    flour

2 tablespoons milk
½ teaspoon baking powder
¼ teaspoon nutmeg
¼ cup currants
¼ cup chopped nuts

Combine oats and milk and let the mixture stand.

In food processor, blender, or mixing bowl, cream together the butter, maple granules, egg, and vanilla. Combine flour, baking powder, and nutmeg, and blend with the creamed mixture. Stir in the oat mixture, the currants, and the nuts.

Preheat oven to 375°F.

Drop the batter by teaspoonfuls on a cookie sheet lined with parchment paper or greased with a mixture of a few drops liquid lecithin and oil. Bake for about 10 minutes or until lightly browned. Let stand a minute, then remove to wire rack to cool.

Yield: 2 dozen.

Approximately 55 calories each.

Fig and Sesame Snacks

These no-bake, crunchy bars, made from cereal, milk, fruit, and other goodies, will substitute for breakfast or reinforce a skimpy one when you're rushed—but the taste may have you nibbling 'round the clock.

½ cup honey
½ cup peanut butter
2 tablespoons unsalted (sweet) butter
½ cup chopped figs (raisins may be substituted)

½ cup dry milk powder
2½ cups Grapenuts cereal
1 tablespoon grated orange rind
3 tablespoons sesame seeds, toasted

In a saucepan, over low heat, blend the honey, peanut butter, and butter. Remove from heat and stir in the chopped figs or raisins. Add the dry milk and Grapenuts, and mix well. Press firmly into a 9-inch-square pan. Sprinkle with sesame seeds and press them in. Cool for one hour, then cut into 1½-inch squares. Keep refrigerated or frozen. **Yield:** 25 squares.

Approximately 130 calories each.

Munchable Orange Wheat Germ Gems

These little gems have what it takes to keep your body and mind functioning in high gear—fiber, protein, vitamins, minerals, and the bioflavinoids, provided by the orange rind, which go to bat for your immune system. The cookies freeze well, travel well, and taste swell.

½ cup oil (preferably olive)
½ cup honey
2 eggs
1 cup steamed carrots, chopped
1 teaspoon vanilla
⅓ cup wheat germ
¾ cup whole wheat pastry
    flour

¼ cup soy flour
½ cup coconut shreds
2 tablespoons cornmeal
    (preferably Hi-lysine)
2 tablespoons oat bran or
    rolled oats
2 tablespoons grated orange
    rind

In food processor, blender, or mixing bowl, cream together oil, honey, eggs, and vanilla. Add carrots and blend. In another bowl, combine the flours, wheat germ, cornmeal, coconut, orange rind, and oats. Add to creamed mixture and blend.

Preheat oven to 350°F.

Drop batter by teaspoonfuls on a cookie sheet lined with parchment paper or greased with a few drops of liquid lecithin and oil. Bake for 18 to 20 minutes.

Yield: 3 dozen.

Approximately 65 calories each.

Tahini Oatmeal Walnut Cookies

Tahini, made from sesame seeds and available in specialty food shops and many supermarkets, is an excellent source of essential fatty acids, so important to smooth beautiful skin, healthy hair, and to preventing damaging deposits of cholesterol. These cookies have long been a favorite in our cookie jar; they also freeze and travel like troupers.

6 tablespoons tahini
½ cup honey
½ teaspoon cinnamon

½ cup chopped walnuts
1 cup rolled oats

Preheat oven to 325°F.

In a medium-sized mixing bowl, stir tahini and honey together. Add the nuts, then the oatmeal sprinkled with the cinnamon, and mix to blend ingredients.

Drop the batter by teaspoonfuls on a cookie sheet lined with parchment paper or greased with a few drops of liquid lecithin and oil. Bake for 10 to 12 minutes.

Yield: 2½ to 3 dozen.

Approximately 40 calories each.

IN PRAISE OF VEGETABLES

Many years ago a cartoon in the *New Yorker* depicted a small, grumpy little girl glowering at her dinner plate. "I say it's spinach," she said, "and I say the hell with it."

That pretty much sums up most children's and many adults' attitude toward vegetables.

You can tell veggie-avoiders from now till tomorrow that vegetables, both raw and cooked, are storehouses of vitamins and minerals, that they are high-fiber, low-calorie, low-fat, and rich in complex carbohydrates, that they contain substances that seem to deter the development of cancer, that they are knights in shiny multicolored armor that can protect us from some life-threatening conditions. And what do you get? A hoarse voice and a pile of leftovers.

Relax! With these delicious cookies, you'll never again have to lecture, nag or beg. They'll eat their vegetables and love every bite.

Golden Carrot Molasses Gems

Carrots, with their rich payload of carotene—now recognized as an important anti-cancer agent—team up with oats, bran, and wheat germ to make these cookies the perfect high-fiber munch.

⅓ cup vegetable oil (preferably olive)	2 tablespoons rice polish or soy flour
⅓ cup molasses	½ teaspoon baking powder
1 egg	1 teaspoon baking soda
1 teaspoon vanilla	½ teaspoon nutmeg
1 cup grated raw carrots	1 teaspoon cinnamon
½ cup whole wheat pastry flour	¼ cup dry milk powder
¼ cup wheat germ	⅔ cup raisins
2 tablespoons bran	1¼ cups rolled oats

In food processor, blender, or mixing bowl, combine oil, molasses, egg, and vanilla. Blend until smooth and creamy. Add carrots, and blend.

Combine the wheat flour, wheat germ, bran, rice polish or soy flour, baking powder, baking soda, nutmeg, cinnamon, and milk powder. Add to the carrot mixture. Blend briefly until incorporated. Stir in the raisins and the oats.

Preheat oven to 350°F.

Drop the batter by tablespoonfuls onto a cookie sheet lined with parchment paper or greased with a mixture of liquid lecithin and oil. Bake for 12 to 15 minutes.

Yield: 3 dozen.

Approximately 60 calories each.

Zucchini-Spice Squares

Zucchini lovers—and veggie avoiders—never had it so good. Sprouting the garbanzo beans causes an explosion of nutrients and the development of vitamin B12, which is very rare in vegetables. The flour, made by grinding the dried sprouts in a seed mill or coffee grinder, makes these low-calorie confections a high-energy food. The combination of grains and beans greatly enhances the biological value of the protein.

1 egg
4 tablespoons unsalted (sweet)
    butter
¼ cup honey
1½ teaspoons vanilla
1 cup grated zucchini
1 cup whole wheat pastry
    flour, minus 2 tablespoons
2 tablespoons wheat germ

2 tablespoons soy flour or
    flour made from dried
    garbanzo sprouts
    (instructions follow)
1 teaspoon baking powder
1½ teaspoons cinnamon
¼ teaspoon ginger
¼ teaspoon nutmeg
½ cup chopped nuts

Preheat oven to 350°F.

In food processor, blender, or mixing bowl, blend egg, butter, honey, and vanilla until smooth and creamy. Add the zucchini and mix to combine. In a bowl, combine flour, wheat germ, soy or garbanzo bean flour, baking powder, cinnamon, ginger, and nutmeg. Mix to blend ingredients. Stir in the nuts.

Spread the batter in a 9-inch-square baking dish, lined with parchment paper or greased with a few drops of liquid lecithin and oil.

Bake for 30 minutes. Cut into 1½-inch squares.
Yield: 25 squares.
Approximately 65 calories each.

SPROUTED GARBANZO BEAN FLOUR

Soak ½ cup garbanzo beans in about 2 cups of water overnight. Next morning, pour off the water. (Save it and use it in soup—it contains valuable vitamins and minerals.) Rinse the beans and spread them out in a colander. Dampen a dish towel or two layers of paper towels, and place over the beans. Slip the whole thing into a plastic bag to retain moisture, but leave it open at one end to ensure a source of oxygen.

Remove the covering and rinse the beans several times a day. In two or three days, you will have sprouted garbanzos.

To make the flour, spread the sprouted garbanzos out on a baking sheet and then dry them in a gas oven by the heat of the pilot light or in an electric oven heated to 250°F, then turned off. Don't put the beans in the oven until you turn it off. Leave them for about 6 hours. If they are not thoroughly dried, remove them from the oven and raise the temperature again to 250°F, turn off the oven, and repeat.

When the sprouted beans are thoroughly dried, grind them in a seed mill, blender, or food processor.

Halloween Pumpkin-Raisin Goodies

Your kids might choose to stay home for these instead of hazarding the Trick or Treat route. Try serving these at your own Halloween party—the results will surprise you!

4 tablespoons butter	½ cup rolled oats
¼ cup honey	1 teaspoon baking soda
1 egg	1 teaspoon cinnamon
1 teaspoon vanilla	½ teaspoon ginger
1 cup canned or pureed cooked pumpkin	½ teaspoon nutmeg
1 cup whole wheat pastry flour	¾ cup raisins
½ cup wheat germ	½ cup pecans or walnuts, chopped

Preheat oven to 350°F.

In food processor, blender, or mixing bowl, blend together the butter, honey, egg, and vanilla. Add pumpkin and blend to incorporate. In a bowl, combine flour, wheat germ, rolled oats, baking soda, cinnamon, ginger, and nutmeg. Mix briefly to blend ingredients. Stir in raisins and nuts.

For large cookies, drop the batter by tablespoonfuls onto a cookie sheet lined with parchment paper or greased with liquid lecithin and oil. For small cookies, drop by the teaspoonful. Bake for 15 to 20 minutes.
Yield: 2 dozen large cookies or 4 dozen small cookies.
Approximately 90 calories in the large, 45 in the small.

Everyone's on an exercise kick. Walking, jogging, swimming, aerobics, weight training, and running, running, running!

Great—for the cardiovascular system, for grace of body, for an upbeat attitude, for clarity of mind, for improving one's self-image. But beware of the mineral blues. If you feel weak and tired, it may be that you're sweating away some important minerals, especially potassium, magnesium, and zinc. You may also be losing some important vitamins—riboflavin (B2), which is necessary to convert food into energy, thiamine (B1), sometimes called the morale vitamin because it helps you achieve an upbeat attitude, and pyridoxine (B6), which helps prevent anemia and may play a role in increasing muscle endurance.

The cookies I've dished up for very active people are rich in all the B vitamins, and in potassium, so necessary for healthy nerves and muscles; in magnesium, needed for strong bones and teeth; and in zinc, which aids in the healing of wounds, helps prevent prostate problems, and promotes normal growth and development in children.

Whew! With all this going for you, you might not expect the final payoff—the wonderful textures and delightful taste combinations of these Smart Cookies. Enjoy them even when you're taking the day off!

Almond Delights

Just a hint of peppermint gives these confections a surprisingly refreshing flavor. The almonds, soaked to multiply their vitamin values, provide a delectable crunch and lots of magnesium.

1 egg	2 tablespoons wheat germ
⅓ cup honey	¼ teaspoon baking soda
½ teaspoon vanilla	½ cup pre-soaked almonds,
¼ teaspoon peppermint extract	drained and chopped
½ cup whole wheat pastry	
flour, minus 2 tablespoons	

Soak the almonds overnight in water to cover.

Preheat oven to 325°F.

In food processor, blender, or mixing bowl, blend together the egg, honey, vanilla, and peppermint extract.

In a small bowl, combine flour, wheat germ, and baking soda. Add to the egg mixture and blend briefly. Stir in chopped nuts. Pour batter into an 8-inch-square baking dish, lined with parchment paper or greased with a mixture of a few drops of liquid lecithin and oil. Bake for 25 to 30 minutes. Cool slightly, then cut into 2-inch squares.
Yields: 16 squares.

Approximately 65 calories each.

Poppy Seed Carob Confections

Those tiny black poppy seeds are little dynamos of vitality; and a good source of the B vitamins and many minerals, including zinc. The currants provide iron and the carob is an excellent source of potassium.

1 cup poppy seeds
½ cup hot milk
¼ cup butter
¼ cup honey
¼ cup carob syrup (recipe
    follows)
1 cup whole wheat pastry
    flour

2 tablespoons wheat germ
2 tablespoons bran
½ teaspoon cinnamon
¼ teaspoon cloves
1 cup currants

Place poppy seeds in a small bowl and add the hot milk. Set aside. In food processor, blender, or mixing bowl, cream butter and honey. Add the carob syrup and the poppy seed mixture. Blend well.

In a small bowl combine flour, wheat germ, bran, cinnamon, and cloves, and mix well. Stir in the currants.

Preheat oven to 350°F.

Drop the batter by teaspoonfuls on to a cookie sheet lined with parchment paper or greased with a mixture of liquid lecithin and oil. Bake for 15 to 20 minutes.

Yield: 3 dozen.

Approximately 65 calories each.

CAROB SYRUP

Combine ½ cup carob powder and ½ cup water in a small saucepan. Bring to a boil over low heat, stirring constantly. Add 2 tablespoons honey and 1 tablespoon butter and cook for about 6 minutes, or until smooth and slightly thickened. Cool. May be made ahead and stored in refrigerator.

SMART COOKIES FOR EXECUTIVES

Your personal stock has its ups and downs—and, obviously, no cookie is going to elevate the downs. The right cookie *can* affect the way you feel about the downs, however.

These "boardroom cookies" are rich in the nutrients that help you handle the stress that comes with success. Munch a few in both the good times and the trying moments, and you'll feel like my stockbroker, who said between bites, "The only thing that gets me down is the elevator."

Dow Jones Banana Chips

These high-fiber, low-fat gems have what it takes to boost your stock, improve your performance, and maximize your potential. Enjoy them with Perrier, milk, or a nice hot beverage.

1 egg
¼ cup unsalted (sweet) butter
¼ cup honey
1 banana
2 teaspoons vanilla
1 tablespoon water
1 cup whole wheat pastry
    flour

¼ cup bran
¼ cup rice polish or soy
    flour
3 tablespoons wheat germ
1 teaspoon baking powder
½ cup granola (page 190)
½ cup chopped nuts or raisins
½ cup carob chips

Preheat oven to 350°F.

In food processor, blender, or mixing bowl, blend together until smooth the egg, butter, honey, banana, vanilla, and water. In another bowl, combine the flour, bran, rice polish or soy flour, wheat germ, and baking powder. Add to the first mixture and blend briefly, just enough to combine ingredients. Stir in granola, nuts or raisins, and carob chips. Drop the batter by tablespoonfuls on a cookie sheet lined with parchment paper or greased with a mixture of a few drops of liquid lecithin and oil. Bake for 12 to 15 minutes.

Yield: 3 dozen.

Approximately 55 calories each.

Double-Good Nougat Bars

You'll feel like everything's going your way when you bite into one of these gooey, chewy bars that cozy up to your tongue with all the wonderful nostalgia of an old-fashioned nut caramel.

4 tablespoons peanut butter
    (smooth or chunky)
4 tablespoons honey
½ cup raisins
½ cup sunflower seeds or
    chopped nuts (or a
    mixture of both)

⅓ cup shredded coconut
½ cup carob syrup (page 236)
3 cups Rice Krispies, corn
    puff cereal, or any dry
    cereal (chow mein noodles
    can also be used)

Combine peanut butter and honey. Add raisins, seeds or nuts, coconut, and dry cereal. Spread mixture in a 9-inch-square pan lined with parchment paper or greased with a mixture of liquid lecithin and oil. Spread wax paper over the batter and pat it down evenly. Remove the wax paper and pour the carob syrup over the top. Chill about one hour, then cut into 2-inch bars.
Yield: 3 dozen.
Approximately 45 calories each.

T.G.I.F. Almond-Kahlua Squares

The spirit of a holiday weekend is captured in these exotically flavored, crunchy confections topped with toasted almonds and filled, if you like, with orange-fig spread.

2 eggs
1/3 cup unsalted (sweet) butter
1/3 cup honey
1/3 cup carob syrup (page 236)
1 teaspoon vanilla
2 tablespoons Kahlua or rum
1 1/4 cup whole wheat pastry flour

1/4 cup wheat germ
2 teaspoons baking powder
3/4 cup coarsely chopped toasted almonds
apricot preserves or orange-fig spread (optional)

Preheat oven to 325°F.

In food processor, blender, or mixing bowl, blend together the eggs, butter, honey, carob syrup, vanilla, and Kahlua until smooth. Combine the flour, wheat germ, and baking powder, and add to the egg mixture. Stir in 1/2 cup almonds.

Spread mixture in a 13 × 9-inch baking pan lined with parchment paper or greased with a mixture of liquid lecithin and oil. Sprinkle remaining almonds on top. Bake for 25 to 30 minutes. Cool in pan, then cut into 1 1/2-inch squares while still warm.

Yield: 35 squares.

Approximately 60 calories each.

Alternate presentation: Slice squares in half horizontally. Spread one half of the square on the cut side with apricot preserves, spiked with a little Kahlua, and press together like a sandwich.
Approximately 65 calories each.

Sesame-Raisin Serenity Squares

You'll be bullish for these crunchy cookies, chock-full of pantothenic acid and all the B vitamins that help you keep your cool.

⅓ cup tahini	¼ cup rice polish
½ cup honey, molasses, or barley malt syrup	¼ cup wheat germ
	½ cup shredded coconut
2 eggs	¼ cup sesame seeds
1 cup rolled oats	1 cup raisins

Preheat oven to 350°F.

In food processor, blender, or mixing bowl, blend together tahini, honey, and eggs until smooth and creamy. Add the oats, rice polish, wheat germ, coconut, and seeds, and process or mix until ingredients are well-combined. Stir in the raisins.

Spread the batter in a 9-inch-square baking dish lined with parchment paper or greased with liquid lecithin and oil. Bake for 20 minutes or until toasty brown. Cut in 1½-inch squares and remove to the cooling rack.

Yield: 25 squares.
Approximately 85 calories each.

BLESS-YOUR-HEART COOKIES

While all the cookies in this book are kind to your heart—they don't burden you with the negatives shown to be a drag on the cardiovascular system (salt, sugar, and hydrogenated fats)—the cookies in this chapter are a special blessing. They are jazzed up with nutrients that lower the levels of "bad" cholesterol—low-density lipoprotein (LDL) —which is associated with increased risk of heart attacks. And they increase levels of high-density proteins (HDL), thought to protect against heart attacks.

In the same delicious morsel, you will be getting an added bonus of helpful fiber and vitamin E, which has been shown to help maintain normal viscosity in the blood, thus lessening the risk of blood clots which could cause heart attacks and strokes.

And that's not all. They also contain the anti-coronary ingredients of the famous breakfast mash developed by research chemist Jacobus Rinse, Ph.D.

Having suffered a debilitating angina attack at the age of 51 and been given a medical prognosis of 10 years of restricted activity, Dr. Rinse put his genius to work and developed his now-famous heart-saving formula—lecithin granules, brewer's yeast, wheat germ, and sunflower seeds. Dr. Rinse is now in his eighties and recently took up skiing.

Crunchy and nutty, and with a hint of oranges and carob, these cookies are also nutritious goldmines. Enjoy them to your heart's content.

Hale and Hearty Confections
À La Dr. Rinse's Formula

With these delectable confections, you will not only give your heart a break, you will delight your palate. Eight a day will give you all the ingredients of Dr. Rinse's formula in the correct proportions, in a deliciously enjoyable way.

3 tablespoons frozen orange juice concentrate, slightly thawed
2 tablespoons honey
3 heaping tablespoons peanut butter (smooth or chunky)
3 tablespoons wheat germ

3 tablespoons lecithin granules
3 tablespoons brewer's yeast
3 tablespoons carob powder
3 tablespoons sunflower seeds
3 teaspoons dry milk powder
2 tablespoons bran
2 tablespoons sesame seeds

In a food processor, blender, or mixing bowl, blend together the orange juice, honey, and peanut butter. Mix in the wheat germ, lecithin, yeast, carob, sunflower seeds, dry milk powder, bran, and sesame seeds. Form into a dough. If it doesn't hold together, add a little hot water. Break off pieces the size of small walnuts and form into the shape of kisses. Serve with love.
Yield: 24.
Approximately 45 calories each.

Heart-to-Heart Chewy Nuggets

These nutty, chewy treats will delight your palate and gladden your heart. They are enriched with olive oil, a mono-unsaturate, which was recently shown to be a winner in the cholesterol wars—even better than the polyunsaturates, which tend to lower both the bad and the good cholesterol levels. The mono-unsaturates, on the other hand, lower the LDL, which is associated with increased risk of heart attack, but don't touch the HDL, which *The Journal of Lipid Research* reports is thought to protect against heart attacks.

¼ cup olive oil
¼ cup honey
1 egg
1 teaspoon vanilla
⅓ cup whole wheat pastry
    flour
2 tablespoons lecithin granules

2 tablespoons wheat germ
½ teaspoon cinnamon
1 tablespoon grated orange
    rind
¼ cup sunflower seeds
½ cup rolled oats
½ cup chopped nuts

Preheat oven to 350°F.

In food processor, blender, or mixing bowl, combine oil, honey, egg, and vanilla. Process or mix until smooth and creamy. Add flour, lecithin, wheat germ, cinnamon, orange rind, sunflower seeds, and rolled oats. Blend until combined.

Spoon batter into a 9-inch-square baking pan lined with parchment paper or greased with a mixture of liquid lecithin and oil. Sprinkle nuts over the batter. Bake for 20 to 25 minutes, or until toothpick

inserted in center comes out clean. Cool slightly, then cut into 1½-inch squares.
Yield: 25 squares.
Approximately 70 calories each.

Fruit and Nut Gems

A special treat for those who cannot tolerate concentrated sweeteners, these naturally sweet munchies deliver a big jolt of potassium, a mineral vital to the rhythmic beat of your heart.

1 cup raisins	*3 tablespoons wheat germ*
1 cup chopped prunes	*2 tablespoons lecithin granules*
1½ cups chopped walnuts	*3 eggs, lightly beaten*

Preheat oven to 350°F.

In a mixing bowl, combine raisins, prunes, nuts, wheat germ, and lecithin granules. Add the beaten eggs and mix well.

Spoon the batter into the cups of two minimuffin tins lined with paper liners or greased with a mixture of liquid lecithin and oil. Bake for 20 to 25 minutes.
Yield: 2 dozen miniature fruitcakes.
Approximately 95 calories each.

Heart's Delight Tahini Strawberry Roll-Ups

You can nibble these to your heart's content. Tahini (sesame butter) has no cholesterol but lots of unsaturated fatty acids, which help metabolize cholesterol. It is also an exceptionally good source of methionine, which complements the amino acids of the other ingredients, making these confections a source of protein of high biological value.

¼ cup tahini
¼ cup unsweetened strawberry
    preserves (Sorrell Ridge
    is a good brand)
2 tablespoons lecithin granules
2 tablespoons wheat germ
2 tablespoons unsweetened
    shredded coconut

¼ cup sunflower seeds
1 tablespoon carob powder
    (optional)
2 tablespoons sesame seeds,
    lightly toasted

In a small bowl mix together tahini and preserves. Mix in the lecithin, wheat germ, coconut, and sunflower seeds. The batter should be fairly stiff.

    Pinch off pieces the size of a hazelnut and roll into balls. Roll the balls first in sesame seeds and then in carob, if you choose. Or, for variety, roll some only in carob and some only in seeds.

Yield: 2 dozen.

Approximately 35 calories each.

High-Fiber Buckwheat Buckaroos

These cookies have it all: olive oil to tame cholesterol levels; fiber to prevent constipation and stress; wheat germ for vitamin E; applesauce for pectin, which slows down the digestion of cholesterol-rich foods and helps to detoxify the body; and lecithin granules, your heart's best friend. Live it up—your ticker (and taste buds) never had it so good!

1 egg
¼ cup olive oil
¼ cup honey
1 cup unsweetened applesauce
1 cup whole wheat pastry flour
1 teaspoon baking soda
¼ cup wheat germ
½ teaspoon baking powder
¼ cup bran
3 tablespoons lecithin granules

1 teaspoon cinnamon
¼ teaspoon ground cloves
¼ teaspoon freshly grated nutmeg
¼ cup raisins
½ cup uncooked buckwheat groats (also known as kasha, and available at supermarkets and health-food stores)
½ cup rolled oats

In food processor, blender, or mixing bowl, blend together the egg, olive oil, and honey until smooth and creamy. Add the applesauce and blend it into the batter. In another bowl, combine the flour, baking soda, wheat germ, baking powder, bran, lecithin, cinnamon, cloves, and nutmeg. Add to the batter and blend briefly, just to integrate ingredients. Stir in the raisins, groats, and oats.

Preheat oven to 350°F.

Drop the batter by teaspoonfuls on cookie sheets lined with parchment paper or greased with a mixture of liquid lecithin and oil. Bake for 10 to 12 minutes.

Yield: 4 dozen.

Approximately 40 calories each.

RECIPES FOR A ROMANTIC EVENING

Want to keep the magic in your marriage? Set the stage for an enchanted evening with candlelight and wine and soft romantic music, but do your homework in the kitchen. Make up a batch of cookies rich in such delicious turn-ons as almonds, strawberries, raisins, and coconuts. Like all Smart Cookies, the following treats are loaded with vitamins and minerals, such as thiamine, niacin, potassium, and zinc, which help orchestrate a woman's metabolism and ward off impotence in men.

I confess—the cookies in this chapter are wickedly seductive. Try them during tea for two, on a getaway picnic in the country, or for a midnight snack. They might help make your honeymoon last forever!

Live-It-Up Carob Walnut Halvah

Women in ancient Babylonia ate halvah to enhance their sex appeal, and now research gives scientific support to this old folklore. Potassium in the sesame seeds and aspartic acid in the honey provide nutrients that help relieve chronic fatigue and stimulate interest in love-making!

¼ cup tahini
¼ cup honey
½ cup unsweetened shredded
   coconut
½ cup wheat germ

½ cup sunflower seeds
½ teaspoon cinnamon
2 tablespoons carob powder
¼ cup crushed walnuts
   (optional)

In a medium-sized bowl, blend together the tahini and honey. Using a seed mill or blender, grind the coconut, wheat germ, and sunflower seeds very fine. Combine with the tahini mixture. Add the carob and cinnamon and knead the mixture into a ball of dough.

Separate the dough into 4 parts. Roll each part into a roll about 1 inch in diameter, and coat with walnuts if you choose to use them. Wrap each roll separately in wax paper and refrigerate. Cut into ½-inch slices as needed.

Yield: 4 rolls, each 6 inches in length. Each roll yields 12 slices.
Approximately 50 calories per ½-inch slice.

Love-In-Bloom Fruit and Nut Squares

These tasty tidbits give you a big jolt of potassium, calcium, and magnesium.

2 cups dried fruits (raisins, dates, prunes, and figs)
½ cup nuts (cashews, pecans, almonds, or walnuts)
2 tablespoons carob powder
1 tablespoon honey
wheat germ, coconut, or sesame seeds (about ¾ cup)
whole almonds, cashews, or walnuts for garnish

Chop fruit and ½ cup nuts in food mill, blender, or food processor. Mix in carob and honey.

Pinch off walnut-sized pieces, roll them in wheat germ, coconut, or sesame seeds, and press into a square. Top each piece with an almond, a half cashew, or a piece of walnut.

Yield: 2 dozen.

Approximately 55 calories each.

Almond Crescents

A delicious prop for a romantic evening, these melt-in-your-mouth cookies are loaded with crunchy almonds, a good source of vitamin E and potassium.

¼ cup vegetable oil (preferably olive)
¼ cup butter
¼ cup honey
1 teaspoon vanilla
½ cup whole wheat pastry flour

½ cup sunflower seed flour
¼ cup wheat germ
1 cup almonds, ground to a flour
½ cup almonds, chopped

In food processor, blender, or mixing bowl, blend oil, butter, honey, and vanilla till smooth and creamy. Combine the whole wheat flour, sunflower seed flour, wheat germ, and almond flour, and add to the mixture. Blend. Chill dough for about a half hour.

Preheat oven to 325°F.

Pinch off walnut-sized chunks of dough and shape into crescents. Dip each crescent in chopped almonds. Bake for 10 to 12 minutes or until delicately browned.

Yield: 32 crescents.

Approximately 100 calories each.

FOUNTAIN OF YOUTH COOKIES

You can live it up and live longer if you give your body optimum nutrition, with more vitamins and minerals which, as you light more candles on your birthday cake, your body needs more but utilizes less.

How do you do that? By addition and subtraction. Subtract the foods that add only empty calories. Add the foods that give you important nutrients, and you will multiply your chances of enjoying all your years in the best of health.

The cookies in this chapter are fortified with ingredients that have been shown to sharpen the mind, lower LDL cholesterol (the bad kind), improve circulation, and promote restful sleep. The taste? Your whole family will label them winners.

Fruit and Nut Lifesavers

To stay young and vital, you should eat each day something which, if put into the ground, would grow. Sprouts, sunflower seeds, and sesame seeds would grow if planted, and this no-bake confection bring their vitality to you. The lecithin granules contribute to a sharp mind and a good memory.

12 dried apricots, soaked
    overnight
½ cup raisins, soaked overnight
    apple juice (for soaking the
    apricots and raisins)
3 tablespoons almonds, lightly
    roasted
3 tablespoons rolled oats
3 tablespoons lecithin granules
3 tablespoons wheat germ
2 tablespoons bran

1 tablespoon dry milk powder
2 tablespoons wheat or rye
    sprouts (optional)
2 tablespoons unsweetened
    shredded coconut
2 tablespoons sunflower seeds
3 tablespoons sesame seeds
    and toasted filberts for
    garnish

Soak the apricots and raisins overnight in apple juice.

Drain, and reserve the juice for fruit salad or drink it. (It's delicious.) In a food processor, blender, or food mill, puree the dried fruit, then blend with nuts, oats, lecithin, wheat germ, bran, milk powder, sprouts, coconut, and sunflower seeds. If the mixture is too sticky to handle, refrigerate for about an hour, or if you want to get on with it, add more oats.

Pinch off pieces the size of small walnuts, roll each into a ball, dip in sesame seeds, then press a filbert in the center.

Yield: 2 dozen.

Approximately 40 calories each.

Crunchy Fudgy Brownies

These moist, chewy brownies are sure to wow your family and friends. Besides being rich in fiber, they provide an extra bonus of lecithin, which is rich in choline, a substance that sharpens the mind and keeps the arteries clean.

⅓ cup vegetable oil (preferably olive)
⅓ cup honey
2 tablespoons lecithin granules
2 eggs
1 teaspoon vanilla
1 cup whole wheat pastry flour

2 tablespoons soy flour
¼ cup bran
2 tablespoons milk powder
½ cup carob powder
⅓ cup chopped walnuts
Grapenuts cereal, millet, and sesame seeds for garnish

Preheat oven to 325°F.

In food processor, blender, or mixing bowl, blend the oil, honey, lecithin, eggs, and vanilla until smooth and creamy. Add the combined flours, bran, and milk and carob powders, and process briefly until ingredients are well-mixed. Mix in the nuts.

Spoon into an 8-inch-square pan lined with parchment paper or greased with a mixture of liquid lecithin and oil. Top with 1½-inch-wide rows of (alternately) Grapenuts, millet, and sesame seeds. Bake for 20 to 25 minutes. Cut into 1½-inch squares.

Yield: 20 squares.

Approximately 100 calories each.

Mixed-Grain Peanut Almond Squares

The combination of oat and wheat provides complementary amino acids, thus increasing the biological value of the protein in these unbelievably delicious squares. You can use any combination of unsweetened dry cereals you have on hand.

1 tablespoon butter
1 tablespoon molasses
1 tablespoon honey
3 tablespoons frozen apple juice concentrate
3 tablespoons peanut butter
2 tablespoons lecithin granules
½ teaspoon cinnamon
¼ teaspoon ginger
¼ teaspoon nutmeg
1 cup dry oat cereal, toasted
1 cup dry wheat-flake cereal, toasted
½ cup chopped almonds or peanuts, toasted

In a saucepan, combine butter, molasses, honey, and apple juice. Heat and stir until ingredients are well-combined. Add the lecithin, spices, cereals, and nuts and mix.

Press the mixture into an 8-inch-square pan lined with parchment paper. Cool, then cut into 1-inch squares.

Yield: 25 squares.

Approximately 70 calories each.

Tranquility Tahini Fig and Nut Cookies

The tahini, oats, wheat germ, figs, and milk powder in these crisp and crunchy cookies provide bountiful calcium and magnesium, which have been shown to improve mental and physical functioning and promote restful slumber. They are an excellent bedtime snack.

¼ cup tahini
2 tablespoons vegetable oil
   (preferably olive)
2 tablespoons honey
½ cup rolled oats
¼ cup oat bran or wheat germ
1 tablespoon dry milk powder

4 dried figs soaked for at least
   an hour or overnight in
   hot water, then drained
   and cut into small pieces
¼ cup sunflower seeds or
   chopped walnuts

In a mixing bowl, combine the tahini, oil, and honey. Stir in the oats, bran, milk powder, figs, and seeds or nuts.

Preheat oven to 325°F.

Drop the batter by teaspoonfuls on a cookie sheet lined with parchment paper or greased with a mixture of a few drops of liquid lecithin and oil. Bake for 12 to 15 minutes, or until cookies are a delicate brown.

Yield: 20 to 24.

Approximately 45 calories each.

Apricot Walnut Shortbread Squares

You'll find it hard to believe that anything that tastes so scrumptious can do so many wonderful things for you—lecithin for your arteries and your memory, wheat germ for that great vitamin E, fiber for good digestion, apricots for iron, nuts for magnesium. Invite your best pal and enjoy them with a nice cup of tea.

BASE

*½ cup whole wheat pastry
   flour*
2 tablespoons wheat germ
2 tablespoons bran
2 tablespoons lecithin granules
*2 tablespoons vegetable oil
   (preferably olive)*

2 tablespoons butter
1 tablespoon honey
*1 tablespoon frozen apple juice
   concentrate*
½ teaspoon vanilla extract

FILLING

*½ cup dried apricots soaked in
   ½ cup boiling water or
   Lemon Soother tea for at
   least an hour or
   overnight*

*2 tablespoons frozen apple
   juice concentrate*
½ cup chopped walnuts

Soak the apricots in boiling water or Lemon Soother tea for at least one hour, or overnight.

Preheat oven to 325°F.

To make the base, blend together in food processor, blender, or mixing bowl all the ingredients, from the flour to the vanilla. Press ¾ cup of this mixture into an 8-inch-square pan lined with parchment paper or greased with a mixture of a few drops of liquid lecithin and oil. Bake for 15 minutes or until edges begin to turn brown.

To make the filling, combine the apricots with their soaking liquid and the apple juice concentrate in a saucepan, and cook over medium heat for about 10 minutes. Puree in food processor or blender, then add the chopped walnuts.

Spread the apricot mixture over the cookie base and top with the remaining ¼ cup of the crumb mixture. Return to oven for 10 to 15 minutes. Cool, then cut into 1½-inch squares.

Yield: 25 squares.

Approximately 55 calories each.

VERY SKINNY SMART COOKIES
FOR CALORIE COUNTERS

As I mentioned in the Introduction, all the cookies in this book are calorie-smart. They have much less fat and sweetening agents than their counterparts in the great big cookie world.

In this chapter, though, we reduce the calories even further by the use of popcorn flour, which has 50 calories to a cup as compared with regular flour's 400, and by the increased use of bran, which is not only ridiculously low in calories (6.7 to a tablespoon), but has a very accommodating way of slowing down the absorption of other calories. We also use fruit juices as a substitute for the more concentrated, more caloric sweeteners.

Nosh on these delicious morsels in good conscience. And serve them at teas, committee meetings, and parties. Your weight-watching friends will bless you.

Calorie-Shy Miniature Cheesecake Tarts

Enjoy your passion for cheesecake without guilt! Popcorn flour and orange juice enhance the flavors and slash the calories in these scrumptious, easy-to-make tarts.

BASE

1 cup mashed banana

1 cup popcorn flour

FILLING

½ cup cottage cheese or ricotta cheese, drained

⅓ cup cream cheese

1 egg

3 tablespoons frozen orange juice concentrate

1 tablespoon vanilla fruit preserves (Sorrel Ridge is a good brand) and carob chips (optional)

Line the 24 cups of two minimuffin tins with paper liners. Combine mashed banana with popcorn flour, and press a scant teaspoon of this into each of the cups.

Preheat oven to 350°F.

In food processor, blender, or mixing bowl, blend together the cheeses, egg, orange juice, and vanilla. Fill the paper cups halfway with the cheese mixture. Top with a small dollop (about ¼ teaspoon) of fruit preserves or a carob chip, if desired. Bake for 15 minutes.

Yield: 24 tarts.

Approximately 30 calories each without topping; 35 calories with topping. Note that fruit preserves made with fruit juices as the only sweetener provide very few extra calories—the Sorrel Ridge brand contains only 14 per teaspoon.

Lemon Wafers

A refreshingly light cookie with a pleasant lemony flavor.

¼ cup unsalted (sweet) butter
¼ cup honey
1 egg
1 tablespoon lemon juice or extract
1 cup whole wheat pastry flour

¼ cup wheat germ
¼ cup bran
¼ teaspoon baking soda
1 teaspoon grated lemon rind

In food processor, blender, or mixing bowl, mix together the butter, honey, egg, and lemon juice. Add the combined flour, wheat germ, bran, baking soda, and lemon rind.

Preheat oven to 325°F.

Drop the batter by scant teaspoonfuls on a cookie sheet lined with parchment paper or greased with a mixture of a few drops of liquid lecithin and oil. Leave room for spreading.

Bake for 10 to 12 minutes or until they are delicately browned.

Yield: 50 cookies.

Approximately 25 calories each.

Orange-Bran-Nut Drops

Wholesome and flavorful—rich in protein, the B vitamins that give you an upbeat attitude, calcium, and potassium—these skinny cookies will light up your day!

¼ cup cream cheese
2 tablespoons frozen orange juice concentrate
3 tablespoons honey
1 egg
½ cup yogurt
1 tablespoon grated orange rind

2 teaspoons vanilla
1 cup whole wheat pastry flour
½ teaspoon baking soda
½ cup bran
3 tablespoons wheat germ
½ cup chopped walnuts

In food processor, blender, or mixing bowl, blend together cream cheese, orange juice, honey, egg, yogurt, orange rind, and vanilla, until smooth and creamy. Mix in the combined flour, baking soda, bran, and wheat germ, and blend only until ingredients are combined. Mix in the nuts.

Preheat oven to 350°F.

Drop the batter by teaspoonfuls on a cookie sheet lined with parchment paper or greased with liquid lecithin and oil. Flatten the cookies slightly with a fork dipped in flour, and bake for 15 to 18 minutes.

Yield: 50 cookies.

Approximately 30 calories each.

Crunchy Sesame Cookies

A delightful nosh, reminiscent of the goodies from the old-fashioned candy store.

3 tablespoons vegetable oil
  (preferably olive)
2 tablespoons honey
2 eggs

1½ cups sesame seeds, toasted
⅓ cup whole wheat pastry
  flour
2 tablespoons wheat germ

Preheat oven to 325°F.

In food processor, blender, or mixing bowl, blend together the oil, honey, and eggs until smooth and creamy. Blend in the seeds, flour, and wheat germ. With wet hands, gather batter by pieces and roll into 1½-inch-long pieces about the thickness of a fountain pen. Place on cookie sheets lined with parchment paper or greased with a few drops of liquid lecithin and oil.

Bake for 15 to 18 minutes.

Yield: 55 cookies.

Approximately 40 calories each.

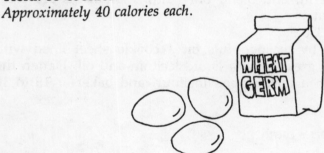

Carob Peanut Butter Meringues

A welcome taste diversion for anyone, but particularly good for those who cannot handle gluten or grains.

3 egg whites
¼ cup carob powder
¼ cup peanut butter (smooth or chunky)

¼ cup honey

In an electric mixer, beat egg whites until stiff. Add the carob powder and beat to incorporate. Beat in the peanut butter and then the honey.

Preheat oven to 300°F.

Drop the batter by teaspoonfuls on a cookie sheet lined with parchment paper or oiled with a mixture of liquid lecithin and oil. Bake for 10 to 12 minutes.

Yield: 36 cookies.

Approximately 25 calories each.

ENTERTAINING COOKIES
FOR GREAT CELEBRATIONS

Here are some sweet temptations you don't have to resist. Every crumb contributes to sociability!

For your big celebration, these cookies steal the show—each one is a mouth-watering picture. Arrange them tastefully on a doily-lined platter and they'll make a gorgeous centerpiece to delight the eye and titillate the taste buds.

Although they may look and taste positively wicked, there isn't an empty calorie in the lot. They contain no negative ingredients and are enriched to meet your high nutritional standards.

For a delicious taste of nostalgia, I have included recipes from different ethnic backgrounds so you can enjoy your culinary roots in good health.

Almond Kahlua Truffles

The ultimate taste treat! The rich, exotic coffee flavor of Kahlua blends with the crunch of toasted almonds and coconut to make an outrageously good, no-bake confection. Make double the recipe—they freeze well.

½ cup unblanched almonds,
    roasted
3 tablespoons carob powder
    plus 2 teaspoons (divided)
1 teaspoon instant coffee
    powder (regular,
    decaffeinated, or grain)

¼ cup shredded coconut
1 egg yolk
2 tablespoons Kahlua, plus 1
    teaspoon
2 tablespoons toasted coconut

Roast the almonds in a 350°F oven for 10 minutes.

In food processor or blender, grind the almonds to the consistency of coarse crumbs. Add the 3 tablespoons of carob, the coffee, coconut, and egg yolk, and 2 tablespoons of the Kahlua. Blend until all ingredients are incorporated.

Scoop up about ½ teaspoon of the mixture at a time and roll between palms into a ball the size of a marble. Skewer on a toothpick, then roll each marble first in the remaining Kahlua, then in the remaining carob powder, and finally the toasted coconut. If you have any left after the usual raid by the kitchen kibitzers, refrigerate or freeze them until company comes.

Yield: 24 truffles.

Approximately 35 calories each.

Polynesian Fruit and Nut Squares

For that "I could have danced all night" feeling, try this treat. The fruit sugar provided by the pineapple and orange is quickly absorbed by the blood and carried to the muscle cells where it plays an energy-giving role.

2 tablespoons vegetable oil (preferably olive)

1 teaspoon vanilla

2 eggs

3 tablespoons frozen orange juice concentrate, slightly thawed

3 tablespoons unsweetened strawberry or raspberry preserves (Sorrell Ridge is a good brand)

½ cup whole wheat pastry flour

¼ cup wheat germ

½ cup rolled oats

½ cup chopped walnuts, toasted

¼ cup sunflower seeds, toasted

1 cup shredded coconut

1 can (20 ounces) crushed pineapple with juice

¼ cup sliced almonds

Preheat oven to 350°F.

In food processor, blender, or mixing bowl, blend together the oil, vanilla, eggs, orange juice, and preserves. Process till smooth and creamy. Blend in the combined flour, wheat germ, and oats, then mix in the nuts, seeds, coconut, and pineapple with juice. Pour batter into a 9 × 15-inch baking dish lined with parchment paper or greased with a mixture of a few drops of liquid lecithin and oil. Top with sliced almonds. Bake for 45 minutes or until golden brown. Cool slightly, then cut into 1½-inch squares.

Yield: 60 squares.

Approximately 35 calories each.

Cheesecake Squares

Sinfully good! These disappear so fast, maybe you should double the recipe.

CRUST

¾ cup whole wheat pastry flour

2 tablespoons soy flour

2 tablespoons wheat germ

¼ cup unsweetened shredded coconut

¼ cup butter, softened

½ cup chopped walnuts or pecans

FILLING

8 ounces cream cheese or ricotta (well-drained)

¼ cup honey

1 egg

2 tablespoons milk

1 tablespoon lemon juice

½ teaspoon vanilla

1 teaspoon grated lemon rind

a few gratings of nutmeg

Preheat oven to 325°F.

To make the crust: In a bowl, combine the flours, wheat germ, and coconut. Using a pastry blender or 2 knives, cut the butter into the coconut mixture. Add the chopped nuts. Reserve ¾ cup of this mixture for topping. Spread the remaining mixture over the bottom of an 8-inch-square baking dish lined with parchment paper or greased with a mixture of lecithin and oil. Bake for 12 to 15 minutes or until firm and a little brown around the edges.

To make the filling: In food processor or blender, blend together the cheese, honey, egg, milk, lemon juice, and vanilla until smooth and creamy. Mix in the grated rind and nutmeg. Pour the cheese mixture over the baked crust, top with remaining crumbs, and bake for another 30 minutes. Let cool slightly, then cut into 1-inch squares. **Yield:** 32 squares.

Approximately 74 calories each with cream cheese; 60 calories with ricotta.

Raspberry Almond Maple Thins

A lovely marriage of flavors and textures, these meringue-topped thins with a raspberry filling and a sprinkle of crunchy almonds can be made ahead and frozen.

3 ounces cream cheese
¼ cup unsalted (sweet) butter
2 tablespoons honey
1 egg, separated
1 cup whole wheat pastry flour
⅛ teaspoon cream of tartar

¼ teaspoon vanilla
1 tablespoon maple syrup granules
½ cup unsweetened raspberry preserves (Sorrell Ridge is a good brand)
½ cup sliced almonds

In food processor, blender, or mixing bowl, blend cheese, butter, honey, and egg yolk until light and creamy. Stir in the flour to make a fairly stiff dough. Wrap dough in plastic wrap and refrigerate a few hours or overnight.

Preheat oven to 325°F.

Divide the dough into four portions. Spread portions on an ungreased cookie sheet and pat into 9 × 3-inch rectangles. Bake for 10 minutes.

In a small bowl, beat the egg white until foamy. Add the cream of tartar and vanilla and beat until stiff. Gradually beat in the maple syrup granules.

When the baked dough cools, spread it with raspberry preserves, top with the maple meringue, and then sprinkle the almond slices over all. Bake for another 10 minutes or until meringue is tinged with gold. Allow to cool slightly, then cut down the center of each strip, and cut across in one-inch slices.

Yield: 4 dozen.

Approximately 40 calories each.

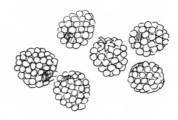

Cream Cheese Brownies

These delicious brownies will remind you of fudgy ice cream.

BROWNIE LAYER

2 eggs
¼ cup unsalted (sweet) butter
1 tablespoon molasses
3 tablespoons honey
3 tablespoons frozen orange
    juice concentrate,
    slightly thawed

3 tablespoons Kahlua
1 cup whole wheat pastry
    flour
1 cup carob powder
½ cup unsweetened shredded
    coconut
½ cup toasted pecans

CHEESECAKE LAYER

2 eggs
8 ounces cream or ricotta
    cheese
2 tablespoons honey

2 tablespoons orange juice
    concentrate
1 tablespoon Kahlua or 1
    teaspoon vanilla

To make the brownie layer, blend together the eggs, butter, molasses, honey, orange juice, and Kahlua. Mix in the combined flour and carob powder. Blend to combine. Stir in the coconut and pecans; the batter will be thick.

Spoon the batter into a 9-inch-square pan lined with parchment paper or greased with a mixture of liquid lecithin and oil. Smooth batter into the pan. Set aside.

To make the cheesecake, blend together in food processor, blender, or mixing bowl the eggs, cheese, honey, orange juice, and Kahlua or vanilla. Blend until smooth and creamy.

272

Preheat oven to 325°F.

Pour the cheesecake mixture over the brownie mixture. With a wooden spoon, blend the two mixtures to make a marbleized or waterfall pattern. (For a fantastic variation, don't marbleize the brownie mixture with the cream cheese. Instead, use the cheese as a topping over the brownie base.)

Bake for about 40 minutes or until toothpick inserted in the center comes out clean. Cool, then cut into 1-inch blocks.

Yield: 4 dozen.

Approximately 65 calories for the cream cheese brownie; 53 calories with ricotta cheese.

Finnish Coffee Fingers

Crisp, flaky and light, they meet the tongue meltingly.

3 tablespoons unsalted (sweet) butter	1 cup whole wheat pastry flour
3 tablespoons cream cheese	¼ cup wheat germ
1 teaspoon almond extract	1 egg white, slightly beaten
3 tablespoons honey	½ cup finely chopped almonds

In food processor, blender, or mixing bowl, blend together the butter, cheese, almond extract, and honey until smooth and creamy. Add the flour and wheat germ, combined, and mix thoroughly. Refrigerate dough until well-chilled.

Preheat oven to 325°F.

Cut off small pieces of the chilled dough and roll between your hands into "fingers" about 2¼ inches long and ¼ inch in diameter. Dip cookies in the beaten egg white and then in the chopped almonds. Place on a cookie sheet lined with parchment paper or greased with a mixture of liquid lecithin and oil. Bake for 12 to 15 minutes, or until the cookies have a golden glow.

Yield: about 4 dozen.

Approximately 35 calories each.

SMART COOKIES FOR THE ALLERGIC

The foods that most commonly cause allergic reactions are cow's milk, corn, wheat, eggs, and chocolate. In this chapter I have created some special cookies that sidestep one or more of the common food allergens. In addition, consider the following suggestions when you are making Smart Cookies or other foods.

If you are allergic to milk, substitute herbal tea or fruit juice.

If you are allergic to corn and a recipe calls for cornstarch, substitute an equal amount of arrowroot or potato starch. Since most baking powders contain corn, make your own baking powder by combining ¼ teaspoon baking soda with ½ teaspoon cream of tartar. This is equivalent to 1 teaspoon of baking powder.

If you are allergic to eggs, you can achieve the emulsifying effect of one egg by combining 2 tablespoons whole wheat pastry flour, ½ teaspoon oil, ½ teaspoon baking powder, and 2 tablespoons milk, water, or fruit juice.

If you are allergic to wheat, eliminate the wheat germ and wheat bran. Substitute an equal amount of corn germ, oat bran, or rice polish.

Here are some substitutes for one cup of whole wheat flour: 1⅓ cups ground rolled oats; ⅝ cup rice flour, plus ⅓ cup rye flour; ½ cup potato flour, plus ½ cup rye flour; 1¼ cups rye flour; or ¾ cup rice flour, plus ½ cup amaranth flour.

Anise Drops

When you feel like eating something dairy-free, but you don't know just what, these nutrient-rich, fat-free Hungarian confections will fit the bill.

> 2 eggs
> ¼ cup honey
> ¼ teaspoon anise flavoring
> 1¼ cups whole wheat pastry
>   flour
>
> 2 tablespoons soy flour
> ¼ cup wheat germ

In a food processor, blender, or mixing bowl, blend together the eggs, honey, and anise until smooth and creamy. Add the combined flours and wheat germ and mix to blend.

Drop the batter by teaspoonfuls on a cookie sheet lined with parchment paper or greased with a mixture of a few drops of liquid lecithin and a few drops of oil.

Set the cookie sheet, uncovered, in a cool place but not in the refrigerator, for about 8 hours or overnight.

Preheat oven to 325°F.

Bake for 6 to 7 minutes. Place cookies on a rack to cool.

The cookies will have a crisp crust and a cake-like interior.

Yield: 42.

Approximately 25 calories each.

Peanut Raisin Carob Chews

A delicious pick-up! Wheat, egg, and dairy free!

1 cup peanut butter	¼ cup carob powder
¾ cup raisins	½ teaspoon vanilla
¼ cup honey	1 cup finely chopped peanuts

Combine peanut butter, raisins, honey, carob, and vanilla. Mix and form into a dough. Pinch off clumps (about ¼ cup), and form into rolls 6 inches long and about 1 inch in diameter. Roll in chopped peanuts. Chill, then cut into slices about ¼-inch thick.

Variations: Instead of peanuts, roll in coconut, chopped sunflower seeds, or chopped nuts.

Yield: About 100 slices.

Approximately 30 calories each.

Carob Kahlua Cheesecake Tarts

No wheat, but a crunchy brownie base mingles with the creamy cheese and exotic Kahlua to delight your tastebuds.

CRUST

½ cup almonds, unblanched, roasted for 10 minutes in a 350°F oven	*¼ cup unsweetened shredded coconut*
2 tablespoons carob powder	*2 tablespoons honey*
	2 tablespoons Kahlua

FILLING

8 ounces cream or ricotta cheese, or a combination	*1 teaspoon vanilla*
1 egg	*2 tablespoons Kahlua*
2 tablespoons honey	*carob chips for garnish*

To make the crust, combine almonds, carob, coconut, honey and Kahlua.

In food processor, blender, or mixing bowl, make the filling by blending together the cheese, egg, honey, vanilla, and Kahlua until smooth and creamy.

Line the cups of two muffin tins with paper liners (one dozen each). Place about a half teaspoon of the crust mixture in each and press down with the back of a spoon.

Preheat oven to 350°F.

Place a tablespoon of cheese mixture on the crust, and top with a carob chip. Bake for 20 minutes.

Yield: 2 dozen.

Approximately 70 calories each using cream cheese, 50 calories using ricotta cheese.

Amaretto Cheesecake Tarts

Just because you are allergic to wheat doesn't mean you cannot enjoy a divinely flavored cheesecake.

BOTTOM LAYER

⅓ cup sunflower seeds or almonds, ground fine

⅓ cup unsweetened shredded coconut

FILLING

8 ounces cream cheese

1 egg

2 tablespoons honey

2 tablespoons Amaretto liqueur

Line the cups of two minimuffin tins with paper liners (one dozen each). Combine sunflower seeds and coconut. Place 1 teaspoon of this mixture in each liner. Press down with the back of a spoon to cover the bottoms.

Preheat oven to 325°F.

To make the filling, cut the cream cheese into 8 blocks and blend with egg, honey, and Amaretto in food processor, blender, or mixing bowl till smooth and creamy. Place a tablespoon of the filling in each tartlet cup and bake for 15 minutes.

Yield: 2 dozen.

Approximately 60 calories each.

Tofu Cheeseless Tarts

No eggs, no wheat, no dairy foods—and favored even by those who can handle all of these. Almond-topped tofu tarts are high in protein and rich in dynamite nutrients, and though they are low in calories, they taste like a zillion!

FILLING

½ cup dried figs, cut up (raisins may be substituted)
½ cup apple juice
3 tablespoons orange juice concentrate

1 teaspoon grated orange rind
2 tablespoons tahini
1 teaspoon vanilla
2 tablespoons honey
1 pound tofu, well drained sliced almonds

CRUST

1 ripe banana
½ cup ground sunflower seeds
½ cup unsweetened shredded coconut

½ teaspoon cinnamon
¼ teaspoon allspice

To make the filling, first drain the tofu by cutting it in cubes and placing the cubes on a folded dish towel. Place another towel on top. Place a cookie sheet or an oblong cutting board over all, then add about 3 pounds of weight. (Use jars of water or cans from the pantry.) Let stand for 10 to 15 minutes.

While the tofu is draining, cook the figs or raisins in the apple juice until they are soft—about 10 minutes. In food processor or blender, puree the fruit with the orange juice concentrate.

Add the orange rind, tahini, vanilla, honey, and drained tofu. Blend until smooth and creamy. Set aside.

To make the crust or bottom layer, mash the banana in a flat soup bowl. Add the ground sunflower seeds, coconut, cinnamon, and allspice.

Preheat the oven to 350°F.

Line the cups of three minimuffin tins with paper lines (1 dozen in each). Place a teaspoon of the banana mixture in the bottom of each, and then a heaping tablespoon of tofu filling. Top each with sliced almonds.

Bake for 20 minutes

Yield: 3 dozen.

Approximately 40 calories each.

INDEX

Ask for these Jane Kinderlehrer titles at your local bookstore or order today.

Use this coupon or write to Newmarket Press, 18 East 48th Street, New York, NY 10017 (212)832-3575.

Please send me:

Smart Breakfasts: 101 Delicious Healthy Ways to Start the Day
_____ $11.95, paperback, 192 pages (ISBN 1-55704-045-1)

Smart Chicken: 101 Tasty and Healthy Poultry Dishes, Plus Stuffings and Accompaniments
_____ $11.95, paperback, 176 pages (ISBN 1-55704-073-7)

Smart Cookies: 80 Recipes for Heavenly, Healthful Snacking
_____ $11.95, paperback, 176 pages (ISBN 1-55704-111-3)

Smart Fish: 101 Healthful Recipes for Main Courses, Soups, and Salads
_____ $9.95, paperback, 192 pages (ISBN 1-55704-163-6)
_____ $18.95, hardcover, 192 pages (ISBN 1-55704-164-4)

Smart Muffins: 83 Recipes for Heavenly, Healthful Eating
_____ $11.95, paperback, 176 pages (ISBN 1-55704-107-5)

Also available:

Vegetarian Entertaining With Friends: 150 Recipes and Menus for Brunches, Buffets, Picnics & Holidays by Simon Hope.
_____ $14.95, paperback, 240 pages (ISBN 1-55704-278-0)
_____ $22.95, hardcover, 240 pages (ISBN 1-55704-203-9)

For postage and handling, add $2.50 for the first book, plus $1.00 for each additional book. Please allow 4-6 weeks for delivery. Prices and availability subject to change.

I enclose a check or money order, payable to Newmarket Press, in the amount of $_____.

Name _____

Address _____

City/State/Zip _____

Clubs, firms, and other organizations may qualify for special discounts when ordering quantities of these titles. For more information, please call or write Newmarket Press Special Sales Department, 18 East 48th Street, New York, NY 10017—(212)832-3575.

jk_bob.qxd